8/1

8/4 504
―――
6

D1141286

Foreign
Correspondents

Foreign
Correspondents

CAMERON BENNETT
LIAM JEORY

Hodder Moa Beckett

ISBN 1-86958-210-1

© Cameron Bennett & Liam Jeory
Published in 1995 by Hodder Moa Beckett Publishers Limited
[a member of the Hodder Headline Group]
28 Poland Road, Glenfield, Auckland, New Zealand

Typeset by TTS Jazz, Auckland

Printed by Griffin Paperbacks, Australia

INTRODUCTION

FROM THE HEART

THE EUROPEAN REVOLUTION

THE JOY AND DESPAIR OF AFRICA

IT'S A FUNNY OLD PLACE

Foreign Correspondents
Contents

THE THIRD WORLD WAR – ALMOST

A SPORTING LIFE

Introduction

Prior to 1988, there was no such position as "Foreign Correspondent" at Television New Zealand. Foreign news was supplied by foreign broadcasters. There was no New Zealand perspective and international events of specific interest to Kiwi viewers were rarely covered.

That all changed in 1988; TVNZ's news and current affairs department decided to base correspondents in Europe and Australia. For the first time, we had our own television reporters providing a Kiwi perspective on world affairs.

Liam Jeory was the first. From November 1988 to November 1991 he reported from Europe and the Middle East as the world turned on its head. The Berlin Wall came down and the communist bloc toppled like a house of cards. The Soviet Union did the unthinkable, and went democratic. The world's most famous prisoner, Nelson Mandela, was released. And there was a war in the Middle East.

Cameron Bennett took over as Europe Correspondent and for the next three years toured Europe's war zones and reported on the ongoing tragedy of Africa in Somalia and the Rwandan refugee crisis. He was there when the Russian old guard tried to overthrow the new, when apartheid died for good in South Africa and Mandela was elected president.

This book is made up of their experiences: not what

you saw on television, but what you didn't see. The stories behind the stories.

Liam: "Ever since I came back to New Zealand I have wanted to put down on paper my observations of the tremendous change that the world went through while I was the Europe Correspondent. There was so much I would have loved to have said then, but there wasn't the opportunity or time. Hopefully this book gives me both. And having spoken to many groups and organisations around the country since my return in 1991, I have found that people are hungry to know more. Cameron and I have endeavoured to fill that need."

Cameron: "My deepest concern on taking over from Liam was that there would be nothing left to cover. He seemed to have had it all: the collapse of the Berlin Wall and the Soviet empire. What was left for me? I couldn't have been more wrong. Those three years operating out of London would be the most dramatic years of my life. Like Liam, I have been asked many times since returning home in 1995, what were my most memorable experiences; what was Bosnia or Rwanda really like? I have relished this opportunity to examine my thoughts, emotions and observations about those assignments, and many others too; to tell of how it was for me."

TVNZ's Europe Correspondent is based in London as part of a joint-bureau with Channel 9 Australia. The bureau is funded by both news organisations and shares the costs of running an office, camera crews, and a permanent satellite link to Auckland and Sydney.

Liam: "In many of my stories I refer not only to myself, but to 'we'. No television journalist works alone. There is always the cameraman, and often a sound recordist or editor as well. So every experience I had, and all the places I went to, I shared with others as a team. Sometimes the assignments were joint operations, sharing the costs and the dangers. The personnel, however, would change from story to story, depending on who was assigned to accompany me. So just to introduce a few of the characters who feature during my chapters: Robert Penfold, Channel Nine Europe correspondent; Drew Benjamin, cameraman/editor; Paul

Boersma, cameraman; Phil Hanna, cameraman; Richard ("Chook") Fowler, soundman/cameraman; Ross McLaughlan, soundman/cameraman; Victor Trofivmos, tape editor; Chris ("Captain") Mannering, satellite co-ordinator; Mark Douglas, tape editor.

Cameron: "Like Liam's, my stories were a shared effort. My cameraman, sound recordist and tape editor shared in all the uncertainties and danger. Their creative and logistical input was crucial; their Aussie sense of humour was indispensible. Every asssignment had its peculiar challenges and required a certain character of the people I worked with. But I reserve a special place for those who came with me to the battlefields of Bosnia; who trusted my judgement, helped me with theirs and never failed me. The characters who feature in my chapters are Robert Penfold; cameraman/tape editor Richard Malone; cameraman/editor/sound recordist Brendan Donohoe; freelance cameraman/editor Lindsay McNeil, cameraman/editor Peter ("Wattsy") Watts, along with most of the "old hands" from the '88-91 years."

You will come across television terminology that you might not understand. Some examples: a piece-to-camera, also known in the trade as a standup, is when a reporter stands in front of a camera and delivers his lines. The challenge is in finding the appropriate "backdrop" – usually a famous landmark or in the midst of action – which shows that we are there, and our opposition is not.

A story is "shot" and later "cut", which means filmed and edited. Then the story is "fed" to New Zealand, which means a satellite link is arranged between the location and Auckland. The cut item is placed into a tape machine and, at a pre-arranged time, the "play" button is hit and another machine records the signal which has been bounced between satellites all the way around the world to Auckland. You can go mad trying to figure out exactly how it works; it just does.

If we appeared calm and collected in some of the world's great troublespots, that's the way it should have been. We can only hope that, by the time you've finished our book, you'll have some grasp of what was really going on behind the scenes.

FROM THE HEART

Melisa

Cameron Bennett

A thin, drained voice echoes down the line. It is 7am on June 25, 1995, and the telephone connection is between Auckland and a shabby, green apartment block in Sarajevo – Cetinjska 13, Alipasino Polje.

Melisa Tolja is 19 years old and weary of life. Yesterday the war edged that bit closer.

"We are very tired because we have been crying all the day and all the night," she tells me in a flat monotone. "We have had much sadness . . . my two-year-old cousin was killed when the Chetniks [Serbs] fired mortars very close to our building."

It is the matter-of-fact, lifeless way in which she relays the details which is so chilling: ". . . a mortar hit her in the head!"

I can picture the scene from where Melisa is speaking – those apartment blocks with no running water or electricity, apartment blocks in which every home has a story of terrible loss. The weather would have been hot. From the Toljas' apartment you can look down on the stretch of road known as "Snipers' Alley" along which cars career at their own peril. You can also see kids playing in the rubbish, their parents setting off again with their plastic jerry cans to the pipeline for more water. It's an exhausting experience; not just the fetching and carrying of water up multiple flights of stairs but also the constant risk. At any time a stray shot or mortar round could land; everyone knows of someone who has been maimed or murdered that way. Most appear to have given up caring. Perhaps Melisa's cousin was down among those kids in the rubbish, perhaps she was playing on the basketball court around the corner – the same spot Melisa was injured last February by a fragment of shrapnel.

A day later I am sitting in Auckland reading about Melisa's cousin in the cable page of the *New Zealand Herald*. No names, of course, just more statistics: "A two-year-old girl and a man were killed early yesterday when a shell hit an apartment building where people were drawing water."

Melisa first came to light in New Zealand by way of a two-way satellite hook-up with Paul Holmes in July 1993. Her broken English, her tears, her hopelessness and her plea for pencils and paper and toys for the children in her apartment block touched something very deep in viewers' hearts. She wasn't a statistic or a flickering series of images from far away – she was somebody we could relate to. She was someone just like us. Her pain and desperation would become the human face of a complex war of hate and brutality, so hard to fathom here.

The *Holmes* programme was swamped with letters, stationery and toys. They were in turn sent to me in London and I was asked to take them to her in Sarajevo. Incredible really, looking back. "We want you to go to Sarajevo." I'd been a year before. It had been the most terrifying, the most intense experience of my career. And now I was being asked to go again. It wasn't compulsory, of course. There was always the opportunity to say "no". But as a foreign correspondent with all that involves, which includes reporting war, could I say "no"? It's a momentous decision – but it's one I and my wife Phyl had worked out some years before. In one of my previous stints in London, working for Worldwide Television News, I'd put my name forward to go to Beirut. But my friend John McCarthy was selected. We saw the consequences. He was captured on the day he was to return to London and held hostage in Lebanon for five years. For much of that time he was given up for dead.

So, I was well aware of the risks involved in covering a war. Provided those risks were calculated rather than reckless I was prepared to take them for my craft – I was prepared for a decision like Bosnia. Journalism at this level requires the absolute commitment to be where events are unfolding. This is how I interpreted my brief as foreign correspondent: to present events to viewers at home as one New Zealander talking to another. To do that, you have to be there.

Having decided that, it doesn't get any easier. If anything, the more tours you make to places like Bosnia, the more hesitant you become. Your sense of mortality begins to weigh heavier. Some journalists grow irrationally superstitious. Famous BBC correspondent Martin Bell wears a "lucky" white suit and brightly coloured socks. It didn't protect him from a gut-wound from shrapnel, though. Then again, maybe he thinks that without it he'd have been worse off. I had my garish turquoise and purple Wimbledon bag. I never thought of it as a good-luck charm, but I used to make sure it came on all my journeys.

I remember crouching behind packing pallets at Sarajevo airport along with a clutch of journalists – all of us chain-smoking cigarettes – as mortar rounds slammed into the runway. It was the summer of 1992. Martin Bell was there too. We struck up a conversation about the dangers of covering the war. He said he'd covered at least a dozen and this was by far the most dangerous. I asked how he adjusted to normality after spending so much time in a war zone. He looked my way, somewhat maniacally, and replied, "This is normal!"

I often wondered whether scenes like that – when we were being mortared or when sniper bullets came so close you could feel the crack – could ever really be appreciated in the newsroom back in Auckland. If they weren't, it wasn't surprising. No-one at TVNZ had covered the likes of Bosnia before. This tour – the journey to meet Melisa – would be no less dramatic. It came close to costing myself and my crew our lives.

It is difficult to convey what that journey and gifts all the way from New Zealand meant to a traumatised young woman in the Bosnian capital that summer of 1993. With me was Richard Malone, the gifted cameraman I'd brought here a year earlier, and talented, laconic New South Welshman Brendan Donohoe as sound recordist/tape editor.

For all of us, that visit, that involvement at a very personal level in the lives of a Sarajevan family, would be a draining and deeply emotional experience. At the Holiday Inn, where we were staying along with most of the other press corps, you could in a peculiar way keep your distance from the war. You could get away from the victims of it and not have to interact beyond reporting on them. You could glide past the misery in the safe vacuum of a bullet-proofed car, seeing but not having to share in it all. But when the focus of our time here was to be one family, and one young woman in particular, there could be no shutting it out.

One evening I insisted Melisa, her parents and younger sister join us for a meal at the hotel. There was a real reluctance I mistook for shyness. But it wasn't that. They knew the meal would be expensive and would rather have had the money. The cost of that meal would have fed them for at least a week. I misunderstood and took them to the hotel anyway.

The hotel's efforts at maintaining standards appeared ludicrous. It is a hotel in name only. It has no power (except by generator), no running water, its food supply is the black market. The windows in most rooms have been shot out and have been replaced by sheets of plastic. Its whole frontage is pocked by small arms and artillery fire. And yet there is the determination here that the hotel should be run as it was before the war. It appeared to me as a microcosm of what was happening outside where people desperately cling to the standards of western normality. On the streets, you can see fashionable women, fully made up, dodging sniper bullets. How do they manage to look that way? They have no power or running water. We didn't either – and it showed! Foreign journalists like myself tend to look more unkempt than the locals.

It was here, among the crisp white tablecloths and awkward waiters, that we brought the Tolja family. They, too, observed "proper" restaurant ettiquette. Ibro and Lena, Melisa's parents, even choosing to leave portions of their meal uneaten. Earlier, they had shared with us what food they had – United Nations ration packs which included Vietnam War-issue dried crackers. They hadn't eaten meat in months. It was their five-year-old daughter, Leila, who shattered their decorum over dinner at the Holiday Inn. Her eyes were as big as saucers. She gobbled everything that was put in front of her. Her parents must have been just as hungry. That they were able to leave food uneaten was the mark of a determined self-restraint. Leila was too young for such pretences. She ate until she couldn't eat anymore, then she was desperately ill.

There is nothing particularly special about the Tolja family. Like so many others in Sarajevo before the war they enjoyed a middle-class life. Melisa's mother was as socially conscious as any in their part of town; her father an engineer by profession. Their "Muslim-ness", as with so many Sarajevans I met, is more about ethnicity than religion. They identify more with the secular West than the sword of Islam.

And of Melisa herself. She's a sharp intellect. Childlike, and yet so very old for her years, she's also the salvation of her family. It's her grasp of English that has set the Toljas apart from their neighbours; her grasp of English that brought their plight to our attention.

The last time I saw her was on a dawn morning in September 1994. Cameraman Lindsay McNeill and soundman Toby Johnston, both Australians, had made the journey with me. Ostensibly, we'd travelled in central Bosnia to cover the arrival of the first contingent of New Zealand peacekeepers. It was also the opportunity to make the drive from Vitez to beseiged Sarajevo and provide a follow-up feature for *Holmes* on Melisa.

We'd come with hearts in our mouths. The journey

into Sarajevo over the perilous Mount Igman had thankfully been uneventful. We hadn't been caught in the Bosnian Serb crossfire that had claimed a number of vehicles littering the side of the mountain road.

Our days with Melisa would be immensely wearying. We were connecting with a girl more brittle, more traumatised than the one I had left the summer before. She was thinner; not just because of scarcity of food but also because of the parasites in her gut. She was desperate in her need to tell of her and the community's plight. In her there was no lightness of being, no flip jokes, no coquettishness. She clung to us, the stories tumbling out one after another. Her own stories and stories translated on behalf of her parents. No sooner had we absorbed one tragedy than it would be outdone by another even more miserable. This friend or that who had been killed recently. We were her channel to the outside world and she needed for her story to be told before she too was killed.

It was an emotional overload. It was exhausting. How could I possibly absorb it all? And not just that – there were our own contingencies. The constant sense of responsibility for my crew, the extreme difficulties in attempting to simply arrange editing and feeding of stories. And at the back of all our minds, the dangerous return journey over Mount Igman.

Our way of escape was to joke outrageously. That and turn the music on our car cassette up as loud as possible. To escape the fear of being shot while thrashing down the rutted Igman road in our Land-Rover on the way in, we sang our heads off – the music was so loud the speakers were distorting. Marc Cohn's *Walking in Memphis* . . .

> . . . Now Muriel plays piano,
> Every Friday at the Hollywood
> And they brought me down to see her
> And they asked me if I would
> Do a little number
> And I sang with all my might
> And she said, "Tell me are you a Christian child?"
> And I said, "Ma'am I am tonight . . ."

Melisa

If we were going to be hit, it was going to be to music.

We joked, when we could, with Melisa too. For a few moments it seemed the light returned to her eyes. It would not last long. "The world does not care," she said. "The United Nations is prolonging our agony through its inaction. I probably will not live to see the end of it all . . ."

This visit we bought food for the Toljas and some five other families living in their apartment block. We bought up hundreds of dollars worth of food in the city market – the meagre supply of fresh vegetables and rice was very expensive – and took it back to the Tolja apartment. Lena insisted there would be a feast; the sort of dinner party she hosted before the war. And it was. There were candles and the warm glow of good times long gone, there was laughter and talk of how life was and how it will be.

We filmed that moment, the candle-lit faces of the Tolja family rich in their tragic beauty. I desperately hunted for the lines to cover it in my report. Close to satellite playout time (we were editing in Sarajevo) I found them. I talked of how we toasted one another and how we promised to meet again, although none of us really believed we would. Over ominous, dusky silhouettes of the city, my final lines were of how we would go, but they would stay in the concentration camp that is Sarajevo.

Melisa watched that report being beamed out of the European Broadcasting Union facilities to New Zealand. She wept.

Later that night, I met up with Miki Kurilic. I'd hired him as a driver and interpreter on my first tour here. Now he was working as a "fixer"-producer for a British-owned television company. "Come back to my place," he said, and we did. Miki is a Bosnian Serb and has somehow managed to continue living in Sarajevo. He's a former policeman and a survivor. Miki had bundled up his Muslim wife and child and sent them away in the early days of the war. He'd stayed on and through sheer cunning had managed to keep one step ahead. His apartment said it all – the only one in the building to have power (he had his own generator). Up until recently, he'd sourced electricity via an illegal junction into the power lines feeding the nearby apartment of the UN military chief, General Sir Michael Rose.

Tonight he was having a party – there was drinking and dancing and singing. I grabbed a guitar and strung together a spontaneous *I Got A Bad Case Of Them Sarajevo Blues*. It was probably nowhere near as clever as it seemed at the time, but we laughed ourselves hoarse. It was the release we so desperately needed.

In just a few hours we would be leaving. It had to be a dawn departure. We were hoping for early morning mist to cover the exposed drive up the lower stretch of Mount Igman. Just three weeks earlier, Serb gunners had shot off the front left wheel on Miki's Land-Rover in the same spot. He'd skidded wildly down the hill on the wheel hub. Kiwi Company commanders had warned me that 50mm machine gun bullets would rip through the hardened sides of our Land-Rover with ease. We were desperate to minimise the chances of Serb gunners having a clear shot at us.

Before leaving, we made one last stop at the Tolja apartment. In our heavy flak jackets we clambered up the eleven flights of stairs with our remaining rations and money. I brought my sleeping bag too; Melisa had told of how her little sister shivered in the cold winter nights. I remember Ibro's hug and the unshaven bristle of his face against my cheek. He had no English to speak of but he hugged me like an old friend. Melisa's tears were still wet on my face when I stumbled, choked up, to the Land-Rover. Her tears and the memory of that pitifully bony frame lingered like a guilty conscience. It lingers still.

The Gallipoli Experience

Liam Jeory

For most young New Zealanders and Australians living in Europe, making a trek to Gallipoli for the dawn service commemorating Anzac Day is almost an article of faith – more important than even the Munich beer festival.

Like any Kiwi lad, I was brought up on stories of the Anzacs. I knew how they fought and died at Gallipoli and I had seen the movie. But I never considered their deeds on that godforsaken Turkish peninsula to be the beginning of our sense of nationhood in the same way as my Australian friends and colleagues seemed to. When time came around to plan our coverage of the 75th anniversary of the Gallipoli landings, they seemed to assume a reverential tone, almost religious, whereas I looked forward to it as just another assignment, albeit to a particularly historic part of the world.

It was going to be a nightmare to cover. There was nowhere to stay on Gallipoli itself, which makes things tricky for us with our tons of television equipment, lights, cameras, editing suites and what have you. We thought of everything. Stay in Istanbul and fly in and out by helicopter each day? Too costly. OK, forget the helicopter, we'd drive. Too far. Hire some mobile homes and camp on the side of the road? No toilets. Then someone came up with a grand idea. Why not hire a yacht? Big enough to hold us and all our gear, with a

professional crew to cook for us. We could anchor just off
Anzac Cove, where we'd be right in the middle of the action.
Why, we might even enjoy a cocktail or two as the sun dipped
over the yardarm.

My editor back in Auckland took some convincing that
this really was the way to go. To this day I'm sure he thinks we
pulled a swifty. The yacht was a luxury boat for hire; skippered
by a wealthy Turkish businessman and his younger "friend".
We learnt later, over a few dozen bottles of anac, that he used
trips like ours not only to earn a few bob, but to get away from
his wife. But they did prove excellent hosts who introduced us
to some fine Turkish cuisine and truly awful music. Life on the
road has its ups and downs.

So we ended up one of the few television outfits to
actually live right on the peninsula while friends who worked
for a British television station had to sleep in their car. We set
up our mini-studio in the huge cockpit of the yacht and prayed
it wouldn't rain. It didn't. Good old Anzac ingenuity was still
alive and well, although it's only now when I think back that I
realise how ironic it was that we stayed in such relative luxury
where 75 years before so many of our countrymen had died.

I was charmed by Istanbul. It had a smell about it.
Nothing foul. Just a musty smell that I have never experienced
anywhere else – of frankincense and myrrh, of herbs and
spices. My hotel room for the first night opened out onto a view
of the Great Mosque; one of the minarets was just across the
street. How romantic – until 5am. There's nothing romantic
about the morning call to prayer when it's happening just
metres from your bedroom window.

Nothing romantic about the small towns on the
peninsula, either. Small, dusty, incredibly run down. We drove
down a back alley behind the homes in one village to see a lone
donkey tethered in a vacant lot.

"What's that donkey doing there?" we asked our guide.

"I'd rather not say," he answered. "I'm embarrassed."

"Why?" we asked.

"It's for the men," he said in a hushed tone. The town
bike? We'd heard such stories before.

The Gallipoli Experience

We caught up with the first of the Kiwi contingent at Canakkele, a small town across the Dardanelles from Gallipoli itself. Our soldiers looked grand in their uniforms, even though outnumbered ten to one by the Australian troops on HMAS *Tobruk*, which had brought them all to Gallipoli. I mention those numbers because when the veterans themselves arrived, there were 46 Australian diggers and one lone, solitary New Zealander – Fred Rogers from Invercargill. It would be fair to say I felt a sense of inferiority; that this was an Aussie show and we were along for the ride. Was that the way it was back in 1915?

We crossed back over to Gallipoli itself and began to tour the battlefield. It reminded me so much of the hills around Wellington – covered in a gorse-like scrub with steep cliffs and narrow ravines. It was almost impossible to move around the area other than on the designated paths. So, like so many who have seen this place, I experienced the same sense of disbelief that men even managed to climb up these cliffs, let alone in the face of the Turkish guns firing down on them from above.

I found a group of about ten men looking through a small New Zealand graveyard on the edge of the great battlefield. I assumed they were Kiwis – I assumed wrong. They were Australian historians visiting the battlefield they'd spent their lives researching. And they proceeded to tell me how some of the greatest feats of arms were those of the New Zealanders. How it was the Kiwis who made the greatest gains, captured the most ground and fought up some of the steepest cliffs of all. As they described it, the Australians fought and died bravely holding ground, while the New Zealanders made the military advances. I was beginning to learn that we were no bit players 75 years ago.

We then tracked down the last remaining Turkish soldier from that era living on the peninsula. His name was Adile Sahin and he lived much as he must have 75 years earlier – in a mud-walled cottage with a dirt floor, chickens scrabbling around his feet as he told us of the day the Anzacs arrived. He told us how he never wanted to fight. But what do you do when your home is being invaded? Even on this day he said he couldn't understand why they came. But did he hate? No. He never hated the men from the other side of the world. They were his friends. We caught up with Adile Sahin again the next day, sitting in the village square talking to young Aussie and Kiwi soldiers, who looked barely out of their teens, and wearing New Zealand and Australian flags pinned to his lapel.

The Anzac invasion had begun anew. New Zealand and Australian soldiers were out in force, organising for the dawn service and the commemorations at Lone Pine and Chunuk Bair. The Turkish Army was there too – its job was to police the peninsula. For, like us, the thousands of young backpackers had discovered there was nowhere to stay. So all night there were running battles through the trees and scrub that is Gallipoli as young men and women ran, dodged and hid from Turkish soldiers charged with keeping them out. I assume it must have been carried out with good humour – there were no shots fired. And, come dawn, thousands of dishevelled young Kiwis and Aussies came out of the hills to gather for the service, I among them.

It was tragic. For most of the service we couldn't hear a thing, other than the singing. Someone had cut the lines from the microphones to the speakers. Why anyone would do such a thing I'll never know. But it meant the service lacked the feeling for many of us gathered there that it may otherwise have had. So I felt flat when it was all over and I approached Fred Rogers. He changed all that.

Fred was 98 years old and wheelchair-bound. I can only imagine what the trip from New Zealand must have been like for him. But he was there on the grassy field that ran down to Anzac Cove in the early morning cold, dressed in his finest grey suit with his old hat on his head and his medals proudly displayed across his chest. He looked old, certainly, but not tired. There was fire in his eyes.

I can quote exactly what he said. "Seventy-five years ago I buried one of the first of the sixteen who fell on Anzac evening in 1915. That's 75 years ago. And here I am today, performing a similar service, a reverent service, the same as I did in 1915. I'm laying a wreath."

At this point his face contorted, the tears began to flow,

and he sobbed. "It's sad, but I've got to be brave."

I could only reply, "New Zealand is proud of you, Fred." I felt like I had been hit between the eyes by this old man. I couldn't really understand what he had gone through 75 years ago; what hardships, and what memories he must have. But I was beginning to.

At this point the New Zealanders and Australians went their separate ways – the Australians first to their ceremony at Lone Pine. Lone Pine is where so many diggers died fighting over a narrow piece of ground in the face of Turkish machine gunners. It's the piece of Gallipoli the Aussies call their own. Ours was further up the road at one of the highest points on the peninsula, at Chunuk Bair, or, as the Turks spell it, Canak Bayiri.

My cameraman had first to film the Australian ceremony before he could come up to film ours. He's an Australian, and described the Lone Pine ceremony as very "Anglican", meaning white, middle class, predictable and slightly sterile. At least, that's what I took it to mean. The contrast with the New Zealand ceremony was immediately obvious, for not only were there hundreds of young Kiwis gathered on Chunuk Bair, but thousands of Turks as well. For the Turks consider Chunuk Bair to be their decisive moment on Gallipoli also. Where the New Zealanders fought to within an inch of taking the tops only to die almost to a man, fighting from behind the bodies of their fallen comrades, so too did the Turks come within an ace of losing the campaign there and then. So it was an obvious mark of respect that they came to Chunuk Bair that morning.

Our ceremony started off quite "Anglican", until the time came for Fred to lay the wreath. Someone started to wheel his chair forward. But he struggled to his feet, this man who could barely walk, and, supported by Jim Bolger on one side and the Defence Minister, Bob Tizard, on the other, walked all the way to the memorial and laid the wreath. It wasn't on the plan. But he did it. No greater physical effort could he have made, and it was obvious to all who were there.

Then he made his way to the podium, departing completely from the script. I remember hearing one of the ceremony organisers muttering under his breath, "Oh no, he's senile. What's he going to say?" I felt like hitting him. But the rest of the crowd was completely spellbound, appreciating what was happening and the enormous effort being put in by Fred Rogers. Again I quote his words. "It's been hard. It's been tough. I have lived this. But be brave. Remember those many memories. And carry on. Thank you."

It was completely spontaneous, completely unrehearsed, as was the crowd that broke into song – "When I grow too old to dream". The "Anglican" ceremony had completely broken down; something "Kiwi" had taken over.

I was watching the soldiers on the other side of the memorial, stiffly to attention while all this was going on. I remember vividly looking at the eyes of the impressive sergeant-major as he looked over to his commanding officer and raised his eyebrows. He must have been given the nod because he turned and muttered something to the soldiers, whereupon they broke ranks, gathered in front of the memorial and, joined by many of the young Kiwis looking on, they all took off their shirts and did the haka to end all hakas.

The ground literally shook. Their feet stamped up the dust. People openly cried as they watched. And the Turks seemed amazed and moved by what was happening.

It took a while for the emotions to die down. And no-one wanted to leave. Large numbers of people simply sat on the ground absorbing the atmosphere. Many of the younger folk made a beeline for Fred Rogers and sat around him in a semi-circle while he held court and told them what had happened here 75 years ago. I found it hard to leave, yet had to knowing I had come to Gallipoli for this very experience and it was time to go and prepare my report on it.

It was left to my Australian colleague, Drew, to put it better than I could. As we walked down the hill from Chunuk Bair he said to me, "I always thought we Aussies and Kiwis were fairly similar – you know, same stock, same people. But after what I just saw up here I know we're not the same at all. And right now, today, I think I'd rather be a Kiwi."

Mission Completed

Cameron Bennett

During the 50-year commemorations of the Second World War, British commentators observed that its great campaigns are largely forgotten by and irrelevant to generations born after 1945; that the war is perceived now, by those too young to remember, for its global rather than national significance; that its enduring symbols are not the Battle of Britain or the fight for the Western Desert, but Auschwitz and Hiroshima.

As kids, the war was never forgotten in our household; it was too much a part of my parents' experience. There were the '40s-era songs Mum sang around the bonfires at the bach. There were the stories of the US Marines' arrival in Wellington; of Dad fitting out their landing craft for the bloody assaults on the likes of Guadalcanal; of Uncle John having his legs shattered by a mine in the Italian campaign; of the skeletal survivors of the Burma railway; of the troopships leaving and finally coming home; of the fun and fear and indomitable way in which the home fires were kept burning. How many times did we watch the old campaigners marching up Picton Street, Howick, on Anzac Day, their medals glinting in the morning sun? And those bleak, rainswept Anzac dawn parades at the cenotaph outside the Auckland museum; Dad, my brother Dave and me goosebumpy from the immense significance of it all and shivering from the cold as the bugle belted out the mournful and evocative strains of the Last Post.

Names like Tobruk and Alamein were household names to us. Just as the Somme and Ypres were kept alive through the stories prised from my great-uncles.

In October 1992 I was sent to cover the 50th anniversary of the great Battle of Alamein; it was a privilege.

I had, in my mind's eye, always seen El Alamein as a place of lonely isolation in the Western Desert. It had always appeared that way in the flickering black and white of the Pathe newsreels. It did turn out to be an unremarkable spot on the map, about 100km down the coastal road from Alexandria. But if it was isolated desert five decades before, now the route was lined with tacky beach houses; its Mediterranean coastline is the playground for Egypt's elite.

I was there with Channel 9's Robert Penfold, our bureau videotape editor Mark Douglas and cameraman Richard Malone. My job was to follow the 150 or so New Zealand veterans who'd come back one last time to honour the comrades and mates who never made it home. They were just a handful; overall some 5000 Allied and Axis veterans had returned to this place, busload upon busload of them.

Alamein itself is little more than a main street lined with flat-roofed houses and shops. It's dusty and time-worn. Carts pulled by donkeys shuffle by; barely roadworthy trucks belch diesel fumes while kids kick footballs in the side-streets. There is the mosque with its white-washed minaret and there's still the old railway siding; apart from that, the landscape shared little resemblance with that of the veterans' fading memories.

But if you cast your eyes out to the shimmering horizon, away from the steady march of high-tension pylons and the resort developments, you can see again how it was.

Out there is still the Ruweisat Ridge, or Ruin Ridge as it was known to the men of the New Zealand Division. Ruin Ridge where, in July 1942, the New Zealanders lost 83 officers and 1322 men, mostly taken prisoner, in just one day's fighting. A week later, they again suffered heavily at nearby El Mreir. The white headstones in the Commonwealth War Memorial Cemetery, with their ferns and their ranks and serial numbers, tell the story.

The commemoration was an enormous undertaking; twin German and Commonwealth ceremonies attended by world leaders and the thousands of old warriors. But, for me, it was the small, impromptu commemorations off to the side which were the ones that were the most moving.

None more so than one blistering afternoon in the cemetery when we followed an old man by the name of Aussie Mills from Bucklands Beach as he made his way down the rows of headstones. He was looking for his brother; he'd promised he would come back for him. Stooping in his RSA colours and feeling the heat terribly, Aussie didn't rest until he'd found the marker he was looking for. And when he did, he produced a poppy from his pocket – the sort you pin to your jacket on Anzac Day – and placed it on the sand at the base of his brother's gravestone. There was a nobility to that moment which I can't describe, and afterwards Aussie looked up with his wet and faded eyes and croaked, "Mission completed, mission completed." The tears lashed down my face.

I have most keenly felt my own sense of identity as a New Zealander at times like this; felt the sense of national pride that goes much deeper than the sort of nationalism that can ripple through a sports crowd. Again I felt it when we filmed our old Diggers as they marched under the New Zealand colours to one of the official commemorations. I remember walking behind them; these men with their short back and sides and wingnut "lugs" plugged with hearing aids; these men who many of my own generation had condemned as narrow-minded and preoccupied with the war; in the dust of Alamein they were heroes to me, and I was proud to fall into step behind them.

At the Commonwealth cemetery there were other quiet reveries too; men like Aussie Mills, wandering among the more than 7000 graves. There was an overriding sense of sorrow; every now and then a lone piper's lament drifted across the headstones; there was a deeply emotional moment when a Maori woman sang a haunting waiata aroha to her dead brother; that while old men in ones and twos filed through the rows to pay their respects. Perhaps it was just me, but I had the feeling that the cemetery and the surrounding desert had assumed a sacredness. There was one Aussie Digger who'd returned, having never left home since the war. When the bus pulled up at the cemetery gates, he couldn't bring himself to get out of his seat. He was too emotionally overwrought.

There are few assignments on which I've battled so hard to find the words to dignify an occasion like this. Having never known war like these men – the terror of a bayonet charge; the pulverising, nerve-shattering concussion of a thousand heavy artillery pieces – I was deeply conscious of portraying their commemoration with the respect and reverence it deserved. In my coverage, there were moments when I thought I had done them justice. In achieving that, I was supported by Richard Malone's camerawork and the expert editing of Mark Douglas. I have never seen a more able field editor than Mark, or one as fast. Our travelling edit pack in someone else's hands could be a ponderous and inaccurate affair. Mark played it like a piano, and was responsible for editing much of the work of which I am most proud.

We were set up in a mosquito-ridden concrete room not far from the cemetery, and worked late into the night to cut our stories. Because of the time difference with Australia and New Zealand, our satellite playout was at its usual unsociable hour – this time at 5.30am.

Beyond the rigours of working in temperatures of 45C and the long hours, there were also the Egyptians; Egyptian telecom, Egyptian television, the Egyptian information office.

There are bureaucracies, and there are bureaucracies, but this was in a league of its own. On one occasion we had a feed booked from Alexandria to Cairo and then on to London. Everything was in place; lengthy negotiations had seen to that. But come time to confirm the feed, we were informed by the

Mission Completed

Egyptian authorities that the $2000 landline cost had been doubled. It was expensive as it was, presumably incorporating backhanders for the local officials, but to double it! And in cash! We cancelled the feed; Australia and New Zealand missed out on stories from us that night.

El Alamein was one of a number of 50-year commemorations that I covered, including the Battle of the Atlantic, the Battle of Britain and D-Day. All of them, most particularly D-Day, were enormous events. Kings, queens, princes, world leaders and veterans in their thousands joined the parades; international television networks falling over themselves to provide coverage. But, as with the Western Desert commemorations, it was the smaller-scale ceremonies that were the most compelling for me.

A highlight of the D-Day commemorations in June 1994 was a quiet reunion in a village in Normandy between a Kiwi pilot and the French woman whose family had sheltered him after he was shot down.

It was the first time Gerry Whincop of Papatoetoe had met Beatrix deMasin in 50 years. She and her mother had hidden him from the Germans in their attic. They had risked their lives to do so. And now Gerry, who spoke little French, and Beatrix, with her limited English, were together again like it had all happened just yesterday. Beatrix would later be honoured with an OBE from the New Zealand government for her bravery and compassion.

Another commemoration I felt privileged to reflect on was Anzac Day among the headstones and restless souls of the Somme. The motivation for being there was to profile a New Zealander, Simon Wooley, who was a head gardener with the War Graves Commission.

I'd been to the Somme some years before, in the winter months. Mist hung heavy over its soggy, brooding landscape with its seemingly endless rows of gravestones. This was the place where both of my great-grandfathers and my great-uncles had fought 75 years earlier. I'd grown up with the stories of the Western Front; how Sergeant George Gunn, my mother's father, had won the Military Medal there for leading a charge on a German machinegun post while serving with the Seaforth Highlanders; how Uncle Alec Cowie, a youngster from the north of Scotland, had enlisted under-age because he so wanted to work with horses. His job was carrying the bandoliers of ammunition; a bullet tore out his stomach and he was left nursing his spilt guts in no-man's land for three days in a water-logged crater along with a couple of corpses before finally being rescued; how Dad's Uncle Jack Bennett from Nelson had left New Zealand as a lieutenant, had been on the first boat into Samoa to seize it from the Germans, had fought in Egypt and gone on to the Somme only to be relegated to the ranks. An English officer had overheard him being called "Jack" by mates who were privates and who'd just arrived as reinforcements from Nelson. Fraternising with lowly soldiers was all it took for an officer to be demoted.

So returning in April 1993 had a special significance for me. We traced some of the steps of the New Zealand Division. My cameraman was again Richard Malone, and he produced a breathtaking montage of images. It's the mark of a great cameraman, I believe, if he can craft evocative feature pictures from a situation as static as this story was; no action, no people. Much of our work in television news and current affairs relies more on capturing the actuality of a given situation. But in a story like this, there is none; it's all about the cameraman's knowledge of light and his feel for composition, his craftsmanship. The challenge for me was to complement those pictures with a script.

The spring sunshine and gently rolling fields of crops of the Somme are deceptive. The old battlefields of the Western Front have a benign look, yet you can't escape the uncanny sense of the horror that unfolded here; a feeling that you are treading on bones.

We filmed the sun going down over the headstones at Caterpillar Ridge; the place where in September 1916 the New Zealanders fought for 23 days straight and suffered 7000 casualties, of whom 1600 died. All of that to take just four kilometres of ground.

A lifetime and more has passed since that time, and

Mission Completed

I'm still none the wiser as to why so many New Zealand boys had to die there. And the names on the headstones; the farmer's boy from Central Otago, the apprentice from Wellington and the family man from Auckland; I was left wondering if anyone remembers anymore who they were. For all of that, I also realised, probably for the first time, what was meant by "Age shall not weary them, nor the years condemn." And if, at the going down of the sun and in the morning, they were not remembered individually anymore, their slaughter should never be forgotten.

There was another realisation for me too; that New Zealand has earned its right to have a stake in Europe and a share in its prosperity. It was paid for in blood.

THE EUROPEAN REVOLUTION

The Fall of the Berlin Wall

Liam Jeory

There is a question I'm asked more than any other: what was it like standing on the Berlin Wall? It was incredibly dirty. I ripped my trousers and lost a button off my favourite black foreign correspondents' coat climbing up on the wall. And yes, it was incredibly exciting. I had a real sense of history being made.

In any journalist's career, there comes an assignment – a story – that above all else you feel is one's crowning achievement. For me, the fall of the Berlin Wall was that assignment, and almost my greatest disaster. For a long time I wondered if I was going to develop an ulcer, or if I would even have children. Let me explain.

I was on tour with the 1989 Kiwi rugby league team in the north of England when thousands of East Germans began seeking refuge in Hungary and Czechoslovakia, hoping to find a way to the West. Citizens within East Germany were taking to the streets and the government of Erich Honecker was going to have to yield. The crisis finally developed to the point where a decision had to be made: did I stay and cover the third and deciding test, or did I go to Berlin? It may seem an obvious choice, but back in 1989 it wasn't. My job till then had been covering events of specific interest to New Zealand, leaving the big European developments to the big international news organisations. So it was a sea change of sorts when the word came from Auckland – drop the league, get to Berlin. I really felt like an international foreign correspondent.

No-one quite knew what was going to happen – just that something had to blow. I flew to Berlin with Robert Penfold, the bureau chief for Channel Nine, cameraman Paul Boersma, sound operator Ross McLaughlan and editor Vic Trofivmos . . . and what seemed like half the world's media, all trying to talk in louder voices than each other. Some had so much equipment that planes were flying out with cargo holds full but, because of the weight, empty seats. So extra flights were laid on just to get the media to Berlin.

Our hotel wasn't exactly five star – in fact it would have struggled to make two. But it had something better than that. Location, location, location. It was situated smack bang next to the Berlin Wall, about 300 metres from Checkpoint Charlie, 100 metres from Potzdamerplatz and 500 metres from the Brandenburg Gate. As soon as we had checked in and unloaded our equipment, Rob, the crew and I decided to stroll to the Brandenburg Gate to film the crosses of those who had died trying to get over the wall. We arrived at around half past five in the evening – the precise moment that West Germans took it into their heads to climb on top of the wall. Brave journalists that we were, we waited for the gunfire – there was none – and then there was no holding us back.

Now every journalist who was there that day would claim to be the first on the wall. Suffice to say I climbed on the wall within minutes of the invasion; enough to be able to say that I was there at the pivotal moment that communism died. This is why:

Lined up on the inside curve of the wall were dozens of East German border guards, in immaculate uniforms, AK-47s held high, trying to face hundreds of mostly young West Germans jeering down at them. These guards had killed some one hundred people in the 28-year history of the wall, often for a lot less than just standing on it. Would they do the same now?

The Fall of the Berlin Wall

The East German side of the wall was pristine white in contrast to the West German side, which was covered in graffiti. I watched – indeed filmed – as a young West German reached into his coat pocket, pulled out an aerosol paint can, shook it, reached over and started to spray on the East German side. What really mattered was that the East German border guards did nothing, they just watched. And I remember thinking, "If these guards can't stop a graffiti artist, they sure as heck can't stop millions of their own people from getting out." It was as significant as the first brick that toppled later that evening.

It was not the East Germans who forced us down off the wall that late afternoon, it was the smiling West German police. And for my part, I knew that I had just witnessed a tremendous moment in world history – indeed, been part of it. The footage we had shot was priceless and, more to the point, exclusive, for I saw only one other television film crew with us on the wall at that time.

We rushed back to our hotel, as you would imagine, in a high state of excitement.

But time was against us. We had but an hour to write and edit our stories if we were to have any hope of getting them sent to New Zealand and Australia in time for the news. The writing wasn't a problem; stories like this virtually write themselves. It was the actual editing – turning our priceless prose and pictures into the finished product. It would normally take at least an hour to edit each of our stories. We had two to do, and still only one hour.

Our Aussie editor, Victor Trofivmos, rose to the occasion. He took one look at two hyperventilating journalists and, with a slow and deliberate manner, pulled on his prized blue jersey, turned his blue cap back on his head, put out an arm and snapped "Beer." Hand clasped firmly around Berlin's finest pilsener, he took a sip, carefully placed the can on the table and pronounced, "The People's Editor is ready."

For the next 45 minutes he was a blur; Rob and I running into oxygen debt and looking at our watches. But the People's Editor finished his work in what I still believe was world record time. Then he finished the beer.

Now our troubles began anew. We had only half an hour to find the local Berlin television station through which we could send our stories back to New Zealand and Australia. None of us spoke German, let alone read German street maps.

Now I hope Robert Penfold will forgive me for saying that he's a scary driver at the best of times. Rushing blindly though dark Berlin streets, completely lost, he was terrifying. I could feel myself lapsing into a blind panic as we took yet another wrong turning, found yet another dead end street. But somehow he got us there on time . . . which is when everything fell apart. The television station was under siege! It seemed like every television organisation in the world had descended, journalists clutching their finest moments in hand and all demanding that they be send back to CBS, ABC and NBC in America, to BBC and ITN in London, to CBC Canada and NHK Japan. You can imagine where TVNZ Auckland came in the priorities of that lot. Not very high.

And in the middle of it all was a lone operations manager trying to meet everyone's demands, and unable to satisfy any. You see, there was only one satellite link available out of Berlin at that moment, and it had been block booked by one of the American networks. And with the nighttime assault on the wall about to get under way, understandably it wasn't allowing anyone else to use it.

We had managed to prearrange a satellite link. But in the pressure and chaos, nothing seemed to go right. Someone in a European control room somewhere didn't flick a switch in time and my story ended up being sent to Portugal. Then friends of mine from Globo Television in Brazil, seeing my dilemma, said they had three minutes left on their satellite feed, and we could use that. So half of my story was sent to Rio de Janeiro before that satellite time ran out too. I was left with the option of telling Television New Zealand to retrieve half my story from Portugal and the other half from Brazil.

I watched grown men and women slumped in corridors crying with rage and frustration; shouting threats, offering bribes, anything if the operations manager could just find a way out. By way of analogy, it would be like a McLaren racing team descending on a mechanic in Eketahuna and demand he fix their blown engine. I could not believe this was happening to me. Having stood on the wall at that climactic moment, having reported it, now stymied at this point . . . not only did my career flash before my eyes, but some very unprintable thoughts as well.

I wish I could lay claim to finding a way out of the impasse, for saving my own career. But for that I have to thank our own satellite operations manager back in the TVNZ/Channel Nine bureau in London. Chris Mannering (Captain Mainwaring, as we call him) had a heck of a record – he had never failed to find a way of getting our material out of wherever in the world we happened to be. And he wasn't about to let his 100 per cent record be broken on the biggest story of the decade.

Imagine a tunnel in progress in which the tunneling machine has broken down. Hundreds of people are milling around inside, demanding the machine be fixed, now. Chris simply arranged to tunnel through from the other end. He organised the satellite links from New Zealand, through the United States, on to London, across to France and from there to Frankfurt. And when he asked the somewhat harassed German operations manager could he just send my story to Frankfurt, the answer was, "My friend, I can't send to America, I can't send to Canada let alone to New Zealand or Australia. But a simple little transmission to Frankfurt? Now that I can do!"

We were a happy little band that left the Berlin TV station that night, which is more than could be said for many of our less fortunate colleagues. Happier still, because Rob didn't drive home. By now hundreds of West Germans were reoccupying the wall, and had even brought in a digger to start dismantling it. On a more modest scale, ordinary citizens were hacking away with hammers and chisels. We joined the celebrations for a short while. I hacked off my personal piece of the wall and convinced a Russian officer that his hat was worth selling. I watched enviously as a personal assistant to one of America's leading news anchors, who'd just arrived in town, held a ladder so his boss could climb on to the wall without ripping his trousers or damaging his coat. Then I went back to the hotel to await first light, and the East German government's promise that tomorrow it would set its people free.

Potzdamerplatz was the place chosen for the wall to be officially breached. We waited along with tens of thousands of West Germans who formed two lines as far as the eye could see, a human sea parted in the middle, through which the East Germans were going to walk through to the West and freedom. As the first people came through to hugs, kisses, flowers and cheers, I turned to look at Paul Boersma – a laconic Australian not given to wild excesses of emotion – and saw the tears rolling down his cheeks as he worked. He'll never admit to crying, but it set me off. The best line I ever saw to describe what happened that day was one I ended up quoting: "Today the edge of the world has gone."

The East Germans, though, didn't seem to be thinking such deep thoughts as they came through the wall clutching their ostmarks. They headed straight for the Kerfursdendamm in the heart of Berlin and consumer paradise. We followed and filmed their expressions; first of delight, as one particular family gazed at the shop windows, and then tears as they realised that their savings could barely buy them lunch let alone new clothes and other consumer goods they craved. It was a crazy day, one that took the East Germans (and, by association, us) from joy in the morning to deep sadness in the evening. They finally had freedom . . . and they couldn't afford it! There were few smiles as the East Germans trudged back through the hole in the wall that night; back to their depressing grey homes and depressing grey lives, and left behind a glittering Berlin to the West Germans who were doing most of the celebrating. And that evening a new bit of graffiti appeared on the Berlin Wall. It read, "They came, they saw – they did a little shopping."

It was a marathon evening for our small team to put together our record of the day. Luckily this night there were no dramas in getting our material out, and just a very early start to be ready for live interviews on the network news and *Holmes*.

And here, amidst this German rebirth, is where the future of the Jeory line became rather alarmingly jeopardised. By now a virtual truck city had sprung up near the Brandenburg Gate, as the world's media brought in their mobile satellite stations, each team anxious to avoid the fiasco of two nights before. Satellite dishes work by sending signals up to various satellites at different points in the sky. Up among those criss-crossing beams, on platforms and on cherrypickers, stood reporters and camerapersons, held up so viewers could see us against a background that included the Berlin Wall and the famous arch, to East Berlin stretched behind.

As I was hoisted into position to prepare for my live report I felt a warmth spreading around my groin. I knew I was nervous – but surely, not that nervous? And it was getting hotter. I screamed down that something was wrong. It took a few moments to realise what was happening. Moving around among high powered beams is a bit like putting your hand in a microwave oven. In order not to get fried, whenever someone goes up into the sky, all other operators are told to switch off or switch away. The trouble is, no-one told CNN as I went up. The CNN technician immediately realised and switched off, and moments later I was telling Richard Long about the day's events and thinking this story better be worth a lifetime of potential infertility. (My wife and I now have two children, despite CNN's space age family planning methods!)

Having seen all we wanted of the West German side, it was time to take in the other side. And, of course, we had to go through the most famous crossing point of all: Checkpoint Charlie. Ideas are seldom original; just about every other journalist had the same idea, and the queue was a kilometre long. East Germans may have been streaming through holes in the wall with the minimum of fuss but the full East German border bureaucracy was at work to keep us out, or, at least, make it as difficult as it had always been to get into East

Foreign Correspondents

Berlin. As we waited, six people squeezed into a small car, we couldn't help but envy whoever it was in the large white stretch limousine in front of us, and in the large black limousine behind us. I got out to stretch my legs and check out the occupants. In the white limo was American newscaster Dan Rather. And in the black limo was Tom Brokaw, also one of America's leading news anchors. Did they have any idea who was crammed in the Honda Civic between them?

What made this foray so interesting is the breakdown in authority we found once we got through the border. The communist government's control was breaking down before our eyes. Where once, as foreign journalists, we would have reported immediately to the press censorship office for accreditation, no-one was bothering with anything. The once strictly controlled East Berlin was awash with television crews and photographers filming anything that took their fancy, ignoring the police who once would have arrested us for filming half of what we filmed, talking to East Germans who once would have run rather than be seen with us.

And we had a similar problem to the one faced by the East Germans a day earlier, but in reverse: there was nothing to buy. I tried to look at the place as any New Zealander abroad would – what was it that caught my eye most of all? It was the Trabbies. The little Noddy cars were everywhere in East Germany, and provided the most appropriate metaphor for what had happened to the East German government. They were noisy and noxious, with their antiquated little two stroke engines breaking just about every emission standard of the West. The styling was fifty years out of date. And where, to the casual observer, they looked like they were made of steel, they weren't – they were made of cardboard. And we all know what happens to a house of cards. Berlin set them toppling. Next stop, Czechoslovakia.

The Velvet Revolution

Liam Jeory

Less than a week after the fall of the Berlin Wall I was on my way back behind the Iron Curtain. It was obvious that the fall of East Germany had started something, and Czechoslovakia was going to be the next to go.

Having experienced Berlin, here was my chance to go to a fully fledged revolution. It was getting hot all right. Students, emboldened by what had happened the week before in Berlin, had started taking to the streets of Prague. The Czechoslovakian government had done what it had always done – suppressed them. But in these times, batons and guns against unarmed civilians no longer cowed the Czechs; it simply stirred them to anger. We didn't have to be mind readers to figure it was about to blow.

Most people, when they travel overseas, have an itinerary, the right visa, somewhere to stay. We had nothing. But with the world changing around us I asked my cameraman and soundman if they were prepared to risk it and of course they were. We would have slept in a car if we had to – an issue because it was coming up to mid-winter. And midwinter in Prague is well below zero. I'd say it was the coldest place I've ever been in my life, and I've been to more than 40 countries at last count.

Foreign Correspondents

But to an eager editor in Auckland, an excuse like "we haven't got a room" sounds a little weak. So we simply hopped the next plane and took our chances. We arrived at a freezing cold airport in the early evening. Visas weren't a problem, neither was a rental car. We drove the dark, damp streets of Prague, trying to read the incomprehensible map, and some three hours later found a hotel with room. Some start to a revolution.

In my job, luck plays a huge part. Some journalists are born lucky. And on this assignment I believe I was one. Here we were in a strange but beautiful country. We didn't speak the language. We knew not a soul. And I was expected to know what was going on, predict what was about to happen, and make sure I was there to record it.

Well the last part wasn't hard. It was all happening in Wenceslas Square, as in "Good King Wenceslas looked out . . ." The day before we arrived crowds had started to gather in the square in a silent and peaceful protest against the authorities for the beatings of earlier that week. On the edge of the square, shrines had sprung up. Where blood had been spilt the people had started laying flowers and candles and stopping there to pray. The square itself was more an oblong, a huge oblong in fact. Wide two-lane boulevards down either side, with trees and bushes down the middle. It was down this square that the Soviet tanks had rumbled in 1968 when they crushed the last Czechoslovakian bid for freedom. Only now there were no Soviet tanks to rescue the communist government.

So it was to this square we made our way to film the second day of protests. It's ironic that, on my way to a revolution, I can remember the ridiculous job of trying to find a car park. The police may have lost control of the square but they were still out in force issuing parking tickets, and towing vehicles away. It sounds so stupid now, but at the time it was a real bother. We eventually found a parking building and joined a rapidly growing throng making its way to Wenceslas Square.

It rapidly became apparent that the middle of the crowd was no place to be. We couldn't see a thing except the back of people's heads. We had to find somewhere high, and fast, because the crowd was beginning to swell into numbers no-one dreamt of. I'm talking half a million people. We forced our way to the side of the square and went into a cake shop.

"Anyone speak English?" Always a good start. And I never have any difficulty understanding yes or no, whatever the language. No was the answer. Another good line is to point at the camera and say "New Zealand television" with a slight accent. That worked. They let us through and up the back stairs. We climbed up as high as we could until we came to a door. We didn't have a clue whose place it was. But nothing ventured, nothing gained. We knocked.

An old woman answered. An old woman straight out of the Bros Grimm. And no, she didn't speak English. But then behind her appeared her son, all two-plus metres of him. His name was Michael and he did speak English. Not only that, but he was happy to let us come in and to set up our camera on their balcony, which just so happened to be almost directly across from the balcony on the other side of the square from which Vaclav Havel and Alexander Dubcek were to speak.

It was freezing on that balcony, way below zero. Colder perhaps, because there was only room to just stand there. We couldn't move around to get our blood flowing. And cold weather plays havoc with television equipment. It drains the batteries in quadruple quick time. Without battery power, our cameras can't film and our recorders can't record. That's exactly what happened. The crowd had gathered, the main event was about to begin. And the last of our batteries shuffled off its mortal coil.

Just below us in the crowd we saw a film crew from Globo Television, Brazil. They had the office right next door to us in our building back in London. Surely they would have some spare batteries. I rushed down the stairs and forced my way out into the crowd, only to get completely lost. I looked up and followed the hand signals of my crew on the balcony above until somehow I managed to find our Brazilian friends. Yes, they had some batteries.

But, they were in a hotel on the other side of the square. Now the best way to describe what it feels like to squeeze one's way through a tightly packed crowd of half a million is to say it's like trying to walk in knee deep sand chanting "'scuse me, 'scuse me, 'scuse me" like a mantra. I hate big crowds at the best of times, and with time against me this had to be the worst. It seemed to take forever to force my way to the hotel, find the batteries, and then find the energy to battle my way back across the square to our balcony. Inside I was panicking that the speeches would start, and we would miss it all because of those damn batteries.

Despite the immense crowd, the main road crossing the square was being kept open for traffic. The traffic wardens holding the crowd back all appeared to be of student age, which indeed they were. From high up on the balcony, our giant friend Michael informed me that he was on the student committee organising the demonstration, and that he was watching from up high to make sure it all ran to plan. Had the roads been closed, the government would have had an excuse to come in with force. But so long as the Wenceslas Square traffic wasn't held up too much, it couldn't use that as an excuse. Not only did Michael belong to the committee organising the very demonstrations we had come all the way to Prague to film, he offered to introduce us to the protest leaders, even act as our guide for as long as we needed.

It seems the fact that we had come all the way from New Zealand, that people on the other side of the world cared what was happening to his country, so impressed Michael he wanted to help us all he could. Had I scoured the city for a guide to the revolution, I couldn't have done better than Michael.

It was called the Velvet Revolution because there was no bloodshed, apart from that first brutal demonstration. But then what else would you expect from a revolution led by a poet, planned by a philosopher and executed by arts students? The crowds impressed by their sheer numbers, and the fact that, instead of shaking their fists, the people jangled their keys. Half a million keys being jangled in the air is a unique sound. To this day, the sound of a person playing with the coins in their pocket reminds me of Czechoslovakia.

Such was the display that afternoon, the communist government of Milos Jakes had to give way. The protest movement had set up its headquarters in a theatre – appropriate really. It was here at a press conference after the demonstration that Havel was holding court when a man rushed in with the news – Jakes had resigned. The whole place erupted. We asked Michael, as his first assignment, to take us to the cabinet offices where the government ministers were meeting. He was happy to do that. But when we got out of the car to film outside, he was literally shaking, and not from the cold. Despite his revolutionary fervour he was scared; scared of being identified by secret police for helping a western film crew. I looked around and saw only a crowd. Michael looked around and saw plainclothes security men everywhere. So he hid in the car while we waited outside the government offices with the other western media.

Once again I was able to share in the celebrations of yet another communist regime to fall. The people of Prague were dancing on the streets that night, quite unafraid that this time Soviet tanks would come to the rescue of a threatened regime. Michael took us to the university and introduced us to some of the protest leaders. Young, idealistic, long-haired and pimply faced, many of them; they looked like stereotypical students. Yet these young people had helped engineer the downfall of a government, and tonight was their night.

Of course they weren't alone. Many of their teachers were helping them, and those who weren't were making the facilities of the university available. So it was at midnight that there were rooms full of young people making up for the fact that they didn't have photocopiers by sitting at lines of typewriters laboriously typing pamphlets and letters. These in turn would be handed on to young drivers who'd take off for villages and towns around the country, spreading the news of what was happening in Prague because, of course, the official government-controlled media wasn't about to do it.

All this time there was a war of words being waged on

public notice boards. Again, distrust of the official media meant the crowds would gather round notice boards to find out what was really happening. It's how we kept up with the news as well. When was the next demonstration? Read the notice board on the corner outside the hotel.

I spent a couple of hours that night sitting with these student leaders, interviewing them and listening to them try to explain to me, someone from such a peaceful country, why they were moved to revolution.

But the celebration was muted, because the government had only teetered, not toppled. The resignations were designed to atone for the violence of earlier in the week. They didn't work, because the communists were still in power, and democracy had not been promised. So now the leaders of the Velvet Revolution were calling for a general strike. In a worker's paradise a successful general strike was the most powerful signal to a government still having trouble clearing the wax from its ears.

Needless to say, the strike was a huge success. And to ram the point home, Prague turned on the biggest demonstration of all. It's claimed a million people turned up to this one. There were so many people Wenceslas Square couldn't hope to contain them. So the crowds gathered in a huge vacant area next to the Prague football stadium.

There were so many people making their way to the ground we despaired of ever getting through them to the front – the old sinking sand and "'scuse me, 'scuse me" routine again. Michael's turn again. Like any good soccer-loving but penniless student he knew where the hole in the fence was. We broke into the stadium, crossed the field, and raced up into the stands to come out on the side, looking out over a million people and standing right next to the microphones set up for the victory speeches of Havel and Dubcek. I could have reached out and touched either of them.

We had witnessed what must have been one of the quickest, certainly most peaceful, revolutions in history. I remember the words of a young student who told me, "In Poland it lasts for eight years. In East Germany it took for two months. And perhaps we write in the *Guinness Book of Records*; just one week, yeah?"

We were mightily impressed by Michael. As we left that massive demonstration, now was our turn to impress him. We had to rush from the field to prepare my story and send it to New Zealand. We made our way back to the car to find it blocked by another parked across the front. Michael started off to search for a taxi. I looked at my Aussie crew, Drew and Chook. "Do you do in Aussie what we do in New Zealand?" I asked. We bounced the car up and down on its springs. So old were its shock absorbers that it started to rebound of its own accord, off the kerb and all the way across the road before we could get it back under control. Michael was amazed, and just itching to teach that trick to his mates on their next university pub crawl.

That night, another revolution safely and successfully under our belts, we retired to our hotel. By now we had managed to find and book ourselves into quite a nice place. It was time for a slap up meal, made all the more significant because it was the first "westerners only" restaurant Michael had been to. Here we could order steak; where Michael normally ate he had a choice of sausage or sausage, of indeterminate age and doubtful pedigree. He was doubly apprehensive because of the waiter, who hissed at him and told him he didn't belong with us.

All this happened in Czech, but even I could understand what was meant. Michael had told us that, in Prague, waiters were considered the elite because of the hard currency they could earn through contact with westerners. The minute we checked into the hotel the staff were on the make. The porter who took our bag offered to change our money for us, not at the official rate of five to one, but at 30 to one. The receptionist offered 32 to one. The maitre d' offered 35 to one, and the waiter 37 to one, and his sister as well.

Only faithful communists got such lucrative jobs, and so, to Michael, they were people to be wary of. We told Michael to stand his ground; he was our guest. And didn't the waiter know there was a revolution on? Thus emboldened, we soon had Michael placing our orders for us, even though the waiter spoke good English. By the end of the evening Michael had even sent his steak back because it wasn't cooked enough for his tastes. If looks could have killed!

I asked Michael what the revolution was going to mean for him and he replied that, hopefully, it would allow him to travel. He told me how his father had fought the communists publicly and how, as a result, he and his family had never been able to get passports, let alone enough foreign currency to travel abroad. Michael's great dream was to see Paris.

At no stage had Michael ever asked for a fee for his services: for guiding us through a revolution, for the people he introduced me to, for helping me, and therefore New Zealand, understand what was happening over those days of the Velvet Revolution.

On the day we left Czechoslovakia, Michael came to see us off. We shook hands and I gave him an envelope, a gift from TVNZ. Michael got his dream; a return ticket to Paris and enough money for a week. And because of the revolution he helped fight, Michael finally got his passport.

POSTSCRIPT:

From Czechoslovakia, my crew and I drove to Hungary, to visit yet another former communist country in the process of organising its first democratic elections. In an interview with the Minister of Finance, I asked him, "Why did the communist government give away power?"

He told me, "It's been ebbing away for years, and sometimes it's just not worth hanging on to any more."

While visiting the splendid government buildings of Budapest, I was accompanied by the government's chief information officer. A charming man, he asked me from whence I came. I told him – from the fall of the Berlin Wall to the Velvet Revolution and now to Hungary.

He said to me, "You are a goalkeeper." The significance of the remark escaped me and I asked him to explain.

The Velvet Revolution

He said, "In soccer the goalkeeper has to be a lucky man. If he is lucky and goes the right way, he stops the goals and saves the game. You, my friend, went the right way and saw the whole of European history as it changed. You are a goalkeeper."

I glowed at the description. Who wouldn't? Then he said to me, "Your luck continues." And he took me to the cabinet room of the Hungarian government, where for so long the communists ruled, and where no western journalist had ever set foot. "You can film," he said, "because you are a goalkeeper."

The Hell Hole of Romania

Liam Jeory

Gaby was 14 months old. She looked like she was a hundred years. But for a few tufts of grey, her hair was so thin she was almost bald. Her eyes were huge, staring – right into my soul it seemed. Her cheeks were sunken so the bones of her face almost broke through. Her skin was wrinkled and covered with open, weeping sores. She lay in filthy, soiled nappies on filthy, soiled sheets – unwashed and unloved because the nurses were too scared to touch her. Gaby was an abandoned orphan dying of Aids in Romania.

The regime, beggared through incompetence and corruption, could not afford the food to give her. Instead, to stave off malnutrition, it had given her blood – cheap African blood. And the blood was poisoned with HIV. Gaby was just one of the reasons I loathed Ceaucescu's Romania.

At the beginning of March 1990 I was told of a British Member of Parliament, George Galloway, who had just returned from the post-revolutionary Romania with a harrowing story to tell. He had visited a Bucharest hospital, Victor Babesh, where he had discovered ward after ward of babies dying of Aids. He had helped uncover a scandal that could only be called a crime against humanity.

He had also brought back television footage of the

inside of that hospital. It was a vision to make you weep. I quote George because there are no words I can think of to more accurately describe the scene: "The wretched of the earth, abandoned by their parents, poisoned by their government, lying there in a peeling, dirty hospital waiting to die, without even a teddy bear in their cot, a toy to cuddle; having lived without ever having had a hug, been kissed or cherished in the way children should be."

The existence of these children may have been a secret from the West, but it was no secret to the Romanian government. Ceaucescu had solved the problem by simply declaring that Aids did not and could not exist in his country. It was, after all, a perfect socialist state. He simply banned doctors from testing for Aids, from researching it, and from educating against it. Doctors and nurses had no training when confronted by these wards full of dying children.

The story I wrote and sent back to New Zealand ended with the plea from George Galloway for New Zealanders to send money which could be used to improve the conditions under which these children were dying. There was no way to save their lives, just help them die with some love, care and dignity. The response was nothing short of amazing. I received a fax the next day to say that more than $20,000 had been pledged in the hours after the story screened on *Holmes*. It was a phenomenal response of such generosity. And it was a response that continued for years, with nurses and doctors volunteering their time to go to Romania to help where it was most needed, on the ground.

Which is why, in June of 1990, I found myself on the way to Romania, to check up on what had happened to that aid. I should have had an inkling from the moment I boarded the Romanian national airline, Tarom, that this was going to be the worst trip of my life.

In 1990, they didn't assign seats on Tarom. We were all taken out to the runway in a bus, let off and then, in a great rush, told to board the plane. First come, first served. People pushed and shoved their way up the stairs and onto the plane, had physical fights trying to get to favoured seats. Old women and polite westerners missed out and took whatever seats were left, while the slovenly flight attendants stood by the cockpit, smoking cigarettes and watching the scraps, seemingly with great amusement.

The aircraft wasn't much better. It was an old Soviet-built plane that shook and rattled alarmingly throughout the flight. Being one of those who ended up with a bad seat right behind the air-conditioning turbine, I landed in Bucharest completely deafened. Could the flight get worse? Damn right it could. We landed just as the Romanian soccer team was beginning one of its 1990 World Cup matches. The entire airport closed down. The baggage handlers simply didn't handle baggage until the match was over, and the one after as well. We sat there in the customs hall for more than three hours without an explanation ever being offered – no food, no drink, no toilets, no nothing. It's as though Romania was conspiring to give me as bad an introduction as it possibly could.

Still, I had some heartwarming stories planned which would make things right, or so I thought. The first was on the adoptions of Romanian children that were only just starting.

Western couples, especially childless ones, saw in the overflowing orphanages of Romania the chance to give loving homes to abandoned children. I was to meet up with Andrew and Helen Gardyne, who were in Bucharest to trailblaze a way through the legal minefield that made such adoptions so difficult between New Zealand and Romania. They had brought with them another couple, Bryan and Carol Clark, who were looking for a child to adopt.

Together we all visited a local orphanage. There were so many in Bucharest they didn't have names, just numbers. Ceaucescu had banned contraception. He wanted his country to be great and to be great required a bigger population. So it meant thousands of unwanted and abandoned children. The only form of contraception allowed was abortion.

I visited a hospital and had the process shown to me. Every day, women would line up outside one of two theatres. They'd be taken in, strapped onto an old fashioned birthing bed, legs in the air. The abortion was done without any anaesthetic. They were then taken to one of three wards, allowed a couple of hours' rest, and then ushered out into the street. Of course, none had cars. They were left to hobble painfully home as best they could.

A doctor told me of one woman he knew who had had 25 abortions. When we visited her, in her horrible little flat in a decaying apartment block, she told us what it was like under such a system and of how friends of hers had died from infections after crude and painful abortions. It was easy to see why orphanages were overflowing in Bucharest.

We had with us a box full of toys to give to the children at Orphanage Number 7. God knows they needed some colour in that drab building. There was a garden of sorts out front, except that the grass refused to grow. The trees had no leaves, and it was early summer. The playground equipment was non-existent. And inside were all these lonely little faces waiting to see us. They sang us a song, a sweet little song that went "It's good to see you. Hello, hello, hello, hello." And then we opened our box of presents. The smiles were huge. It was like Christmas had come, if these children even knew what Christmas was. Where confident Kiwi kids of today would more than likely crowd the box, grab whatever they could and fight over what they wanted, these poor children quietly lined up and took whatever they were given. For whatever they were given was a lot more than they had.

Before we could enjoy the moment too much, our interpreter warned us that the orphanage staff would more than likely take the toys back as soon as we left, and either give them to their own families or sell them on the black market. There was no way these children would ever get to keep what we had brought for them.

At this point the most curious thing happened. The children stopped playing with the toys and started to mob us. What they wanted wasn't anything we had brought; they wanted us to hug them. They couldn't speak English; none of us could speak Romanian. But we could all understand each other. For half an hour we stopped being journalists and we gave those children all the hugs we could. With a child hanging off each arm I remember looking over at Drew, my cameraman. He had put his camera down. He had a child on his back kissing him from behind, another in his arms, one on each leg, tears rolling down his cheeks and a smile from ear to ear.

Andrew and Helen Gardyne had noticed a small boy in the corner. He was tiny; a six-year-old boy only about the size of their three-year-old daughter who was with them. His name was Stefan. The Gardynes resolved then and there to try to adopt Stefan. With his impish smile he was irresistible. It seems he had been abandoned by his Gypsy parents when he was a baby and had lived all his six years in Orphanage Number 7. We left the place with the last image being that of Stefan, holding a picture of the Gardynes in his hands, having been promised they'd be back to give him a home. He understood all right.

But his parents didn't. They reacted angrily at any suggestion of adoption. Even though they'd never shown a care, never visited him, the Gardynes' approach reminded them they had a son. They refused to let him go. They had plans instead to put him on the streets to beg. It was the fate of Stefan. The Clarks, though, did find a child, a daughter. They named her Amy Marie.

With hindsight I can say I wasn't surprised at the capacity of this country to shock and depress me. For we had yet to visit the children with Aids.

Victor Babesh Hospital had been considerably cleaned up in the months since the first pictures were taken. It was encouraging to see Western nurses there, teaching the locals that they could touch the children and not get Aids. It was as though a ray of sunshine had swept through the wards with smiles all round. The place was clean. The babies had new clothes and disposable nappies. The staff were actually playing with the children. It's just that the children didn't really know how to play back.

By this time, Gaby was dead. Hers was a haunting image that sticks in my mind today. But there were plenty of others who had taken her place. And there were hospitals that had yet to receive any Western aid. So we travelled to Constanta.

Constanta is considered one of Romania's Black Sea resort towns. It's a port city with, at that time anyway, a horrifying statistic. Of 700 orphanage children tested, 432 had proved HIV positive. We walked straight into the same conditions I had previously reported on but, until now, hadn't seen. The children standing or lying in their cots, listless, staring; tragic little figures waiting to die. Having come from an orphanage a couple of days earlier where we'd been able to hold the children, here I found myself recoiling. I was too revolted and scared to pick up the babies with crusty sores and wrinkled skin. I found myself torn with guilt because of my reaction. How could I be so judgmental of the Romanian nurses who likewise found themselves unable to hold these children? Sometimes, when forced to examine yourself, you are found wanting. For me, this was one of those times. It didn't much help being told that many of the children actually shun human contact and cry when they're picked up because they associate adults with pain. The only time they're touched is to give them an injection.

I spoke to a doctor at the hospital, Adina Borcea. She told me that, in a cruel twist of fate, her own son had caught Aids from an infected needle. Not allowed to treat him for a disease that officially didn't exist, she was even visited by the Securitate, the secret police, and warned never to talk about it. It was a sober trip back to Bucharest that night; a six-hour drive largely in silence, each of us with our own thoughts, tired and emotionally drained. We arrived back at our hotel to find the city had exploded.

A violent revolution had begun. The night before we'd been awoken by the sound of the front windows of our hotel being broken. All the time we'd been in Bucharest there had been a tent city in the square out front. It was occupied by people protesting that the elections just held had been a jack-up; an unfair election, they claimed, which allowed the former communists back in power under a new name. The government's patience had snapped and it had ordered the police in to clear it up. We'd gone down at 3am and filmed it. The next morning, with the square cleared and nothing much happening, we had felt it quite safe to leave town to visit Constanta, which we'd done.

While we'd been away, the protest movement had attacked the local television station and trashed the place. It blamed the state-run television for failing to give fair coverage of the elections and helping to skew the result. The place was in ruins. Windows smashed, armoured cars and soldiers everywhere. Again, by the time we got there it was largely over and the place was being cleared up. I had an inkling by now that this was one violent place.

At four o'clock in the morning the miners came to town and what sounded like a pitched gun battle began; like an army had opened up outside the hotel. Needless to say I was scared. No, terrified is more like it. The image of the brave correspondent under fire wasn't me that morning. Except we weren't under fire as such. It just sounded like we were. Throughout this furious "gun battle" there was no sign or sight of gunfire; no tracers or bullet strikes, just the sound of shots. Once I got over being scared out of my wits, I was mystified. It was only later that I came to realise it was all a sham.

As the "gunfire" died down we began to see movement in the streets 14 floors below. Trucks were arriving and dark shadowy figures were walking into the square – hundreds of dark shadowy figures. Then the shouts started as they entered buildings, followed by yells and then screams. As daylight started to reveal more the figures took shape. They were men dressed in dirty clothes covered in coal dust, wearing hard-hats with little lights on top, carrying axe handles and various weapons. They were miners.

My colleague from Australia, Michael Holmes, came into the room with the most alarming news. He'd been rung by the front desk with a warning for us all. It was known that we were a television crew; the only crew in the hotel it seemed. The warning was this: "If we were caught filming anything of what was happening, the miners would storm the hotel and find us." Who told them we were there in the first place?

I tried to ring New Zealand to tell our newsroom what was happening and got the most bizarre response from the hotel operator. When I asked for a connection to New Zealand he said that wasn't possible. I asked why not, were the lines full? He told me not at all. I just wasn't "allowed". I asked for a line to London, to ring home, which he did allow. I was therefore able to alert TVNZ what was afoot, and thoroughly alarm my wife at the same time.

There was nothing macho about our decision to stay and film. And it was one we all agreed with. The problem was how to film and not get caught. What we did was lean over the balcony and watch, like most of the other guests in the hotel. We figured that from the ground all the miners could see would be the shapes of heads and bodies. Michael and I simply leant over the balcony and Drew placed his camera between us to film. To anyone below it would appear as three people looking down. It must have because no miners stormed the hotel; no-one came to get us as threatened.

We then proceeded to film scenes of almost unbelievable brutality in the streets below. The miners were dragging people out of buildings or out of cars, pulling them out into the streets and setting about them. Actually, setting about them doesn't begin to adequately describe what was happening. In some cases they were beating them to death. I remember Drew pulling away from his camera in utter disgust at one stage. He'd just filmed a man being pounded on his head by a miner with a hammer. Everywhere Drew turned his camera there were similar scenes until we thought it was going to have to end at some time.

Watching this behaviour in the streets below, I found myself slowly becoming inured to the violence. Not totally, but certainly in part. Of course, that doesn't mean I lost all feeling or anything like it. But Drew, Chook, the soundman, Michael and I almost became detached. I remember a bizarre moment when we started checking off what we'd filmed thus far. Drew:

Cameron Bennett and Melisa Tolja during Bennett's last visit to Sarajevo, in September 1994.

The human face of Sarajevo for New Zealand viewers.

Liam at Anzac Cove, Gallipoli.

**Atop the Berlin Wall . . . the sort of pose
you don't see on TV.**

**A bit of memento collecting as well as doing my
bit to chip away at communism.**

Brendan Donohoe, Cameron Bennett and Richard Malone
dressed for the occasion in Sarajevo, August 1993.

The broken-down hire car at Sarajevo airport, July 1992.
That car came close to costing lives.

How a brave journalist avoids trouble in Bucharest.

The Romanian miners come to town.

Basic passenger facilities aboard the Kiwi mercy flight into Goma.

Drew, Michael, Liam and Chook . . .
and about a million people in Prague.

Negotiations at a Bosnian checkpoint.

The Hell Hole of Romania

"I've got a man being beaten with a hammer, and a woman with an axe. I've got two redheads, one dark headed man and a blonde. But I don't have any elderly folk yet."

"That's OK, Drew. Pan right and there's a couple of old people getting it over the other side of the square. Over by that flag pole. Got it?"

"Yeah. Thanks."

And so we went on filming a smorgasbord of violence as Romanian turned on Romanian. Like everyone else we'd assumed the dreaded secret police, the Securitate, had been destroyed when they shot Ceaucescu. Not at all. From our vantage point we were able to film the organised nature of this "spontaneous miners' uprising". They were being co-ordinated by orders spewing forth from vans with loudspeakers on the roof. And there were plainclothes men on the ground flashing badges, which the miners obviously respected, and giving them orders on what to do with people.

So it was we completed our mosaic, topped off when we filmed young children joining in the violence, egged on by adults. The madness was complete. And just when we thought it would die out through lack of victims, the Romanians didn't disappoint. They began arriving in the square to see what was going on. Fresh meat. Some joined in the violence, others became victims. And the only thing I could observe which identified one from the other is that the victims seemed better dressed. To carry a briefcase was to invite certain attack. The only way to avoid it seemed to be to join in and become one of the mob.

In moments of great stress people do funny things. We all ordered up hamburgers. We'd been running on adrenalin and emotion for a couple of days now and hadn't really eaten properly. We were all overtaken by hunger. We hid our camera equipment away so the waiter wouldn't be able to report that we hadn't heeded the warnings not to film. When the food arrived we tucked into it, while outside people continued to be beaten to a pulp. Perhaps it was our own version of time out? I don't know. But looking back it seems bizarre behaviour. But then, it was a bizarre day.

Foreign Correspondents

Filming all this is only a small part of the story. We still didn't know what was really going on and, more particularly, why. To find that out we had to get out of the hotel. We hatched a simple plan. We'd pretend we were checking out of the hotel in disgust. The camera, recorder, batteries and tapes were all hidden away inside our suitcases. Then we simply marched out the front door. The miners on guard at the doors had been told to watch out for television cameras, but not for ordinary looking tourists leaving with their bags. So we were never stopped or searched. It was that moment of going through their lines that I felt most vulnerable. I'd learnt a long time before that the thing to do was march quickly and purposefully, look as official as possible and don't make eye contact. All but the most senior of officials will usually leave you alone. So it was with the brutal looking miners who barely took any notice of us at all.

During this entire business we still had our interpreter and a driver. It was a simple matter to find the nearest hospital and the lines of walking wounded being treated. Inside, the doctors and nurses were as disgusted as we were so it was never going to be a problem getting in and talking to them or the victims. They were as mystified as we were why it was all happening.

To quote one man I interviewed at the time, "I was on my way to work. I went upstairs and I saw these miners downstairs not doing anything except causing trouble. And I shouted at them. They came upstairs so I barricaded the door. They came in and they beat me. Then the police came in and they held me while the miners beat me."

The poor man was a mess, with his face puffy and swollen, one eye completely closed, a broken arm and huge black bruises all over the parts of his body I could see. His were typical injuries of those who were beaten. I never did see the bodies of those who died.

When we left the hospital we had to run a gauntlet of people and police who obviously supported what was happening. "Why?" I asked a group through my interpreter. A man held up a blank bit of paper he claimed to have taken off one of the victims, the significance of which escaped me. It seems the paper was high quality paper, with a watermark on it. Such paper had to come from the West as Romania didn't make paper like that. "So what?" Well, to these people that was proof of revolution.

Being the only Western film crew in the city at that moment meant we were the only people with the visual proof of what was happening. Having film evidence is one thing; it was of no use if we couldn't get it out of the country. Michael had rung the local television station. Even though it had been wrecked by the attack of the previous day, its satellite room was still operating. The woman whose job it was to OK sending foreign stories out of the country must have been as disgusted as we were, because she did everything she could to help us. Also business is business, and sending satellite material halfway round the world is big business. To send material like ours costs thousands of dollars, and everyone loves dollars. Thus it was that New Zealand and Australia became the first parts of the world to see what was going on in Bucharest that day.

But still we didn't know why. We had only been able to report what had happened. The answer came when we tried to get back into our hotel. There were the miners waiting around the front of the hotel while the violence continued unabated. This time we had our camera out and I approached the miners and asked for an interview. That sounds fairly straightforward. In truth, I approached them with some trepidation. They were dressed in their mining clothes, their faces covered in coal dust so the whites of their eyes and the yellow of their teeth stood out in stark relief. It would even be correct to say their eyes were red and close set; at least, that's the way I remember them now. These men were, to put it kindly, pig ignorant and stupid enough to tell us exactly why they were there.

The new government had recently doubled their wages, then told them that their pay increase, indeed the new Romanian democracy, was under threat because of the protests in the capital. They were told that they, the miners, could save the day. So special trains were laid on to bring them down from the mountains overnight, arriving that early morning. And all they had to do was follow the orders of the men with the badges.

As I finished the interview, thinking I had it in the bag, one of the miners decided to ask me a question. "What did I, a foreign journalist, think of what they were doing that day?" Was I going to be brave and stupid and say what I thought? No, not at all. I was going to be scared and live to fight another day. I said something along the lines of "The Western world believes it is right to fight for democracy." They all thought for a while and then went "Da, da." We shook on it and I went inside to wash my hands.

And so it was we settled in to watch and film an afternoon of continuing violence. By now we were almost getting cocky, and decided to move our camera down from the heights of the fourteenth floor to a balcony on the third. It gave us a new angle from which to film. At about this time a film crew from one of the news agencies in Europe arrived and plunged straight into the middle of the crowd. The miners and onlookers immediately attacked them. We were wise to stay where we were.

But not for long. A passing truck full of celebrating miners looked up and saw our camera quite clearly. Next thing they were pointing and yelling at us. The truck stopped and unloaded the miners who streamed for the hotel. We took off, terrified that we had been seen. We raced for the lifts and went up to the thirteenth floor, not the fourteenth where our rooms were. The miners, pointed in the right direction obviously, rode the elevators straight to the fourteenth floor. They didn't find us but, I was told later, did find a couple of Japanese businessmen with a small amateur video. They were hauled off, and we got away.

Given how scared I was it's hard to explain why we did what we did next. We'd been chased by miners, another film crew had been beaten for venturing into the crowd, and we'd been warned in no uncertain terms. Yet we ventured out into the melee nonetheless. For my part I admit it was a case of if my colleagues were prepared to go then, damn it, so would I. I was the New Zealander, they were Australians; Anzac spirit and all that. I certainly wasn't going to be the odd man out. Never show your fear. Perhaps it was all of that. And perhaps it was because the miners had largely exhausted themselves and were starting to parade around on the backs of their trucks while the crowd applauded.

So it was we found ourselves filming the victory celebrations. One thing that sticks in my mind is what a sycophantic lot the Romanians in that crowd were, each person trying to outdo the person next to him or her with their applause and praise for the miners. Whenever we pointed our camera at someone, the applause intensified. A so-called democratic election had done nothing to rub out the legacy of Ceaucescu. The brutality of his regime was still there beneath the surface, and it didn't take much rubbing to expose it.

By now I wanted nothing more than to get out of this country before it dished up yet another example of man's inhumanity to man. Surely Romania had run out of surprises? Not yet.

I was booked to fly out the next afternoon. It was agreed that because I was leaving first while Drew, Chook and Michael travelled up-country on yet another story, I would take our priceless video tapes with me. I fronted up to the reservations desk to be told they didn't have a booking for me. I had run out of patience and simply slapped all my remaining Romanian money on the desk and said "Are you sure?" Well, lo and behold, there was a seat after all. I stormed through customs and out on to the plane and settled into my seat. No sooner had the doors closed and the engines begun their run up when they suddenly switched off, and three men entered the plane. The stewardess announced that the plane was overloaded and someone was going to have to get off. Just one person, and the three men were going to choose who it was going to be.

My innards turned to jelly when they came down the plane and singled me out. I wasn't treated roughly, just politely asked to step off the plane and told that I would be re-booked on an Air France plane taking off in a few hours' time for Paris. Tarom Airways would then book me on a flight to London. My luggage would be waiting for me when I arrived, I was told. As I waited in Bucharest airport I figured what they were trying to do. It was an attempt to separate me from my luggage, and particularly all those tapes I was carrying. My bags would have arrived in London some five hours before I did; plenty of time to arrange some sort of accident to the tapes.

Except, I never put those tapes in my luggage. In fact, I had no luggage. All I had was the one suitbag I carried as hand luggage, and that they never asked to search. So it was I who had the last laugh – about the only one I had on the worst assignment of my life.

The Final Burial of Communism

Liam Jeory

It was only fitting, having reported on the fall of the Berlin Wall and the collapse of communism in the early days of my European stint, that I should see it through to the logical end – the free and democratic election of a Russian leader.

It had been 70-odd years since the Russians had been given the chance to choose. It is debatable whether there was anyone left alive in the republic who knew what it was like to have a free and democratic vote. And it was only a matter of time anyway. Mikhail Gorbachev may have been the darling of the West, a Nobel Peace Prize winner and author of the collapse of communism elsewhere, but at home he was in real trouble. He'd never been freely elected by his own people and Boris Yeltsin was clearly the favourite.

I flew into Moscow in no doubt who was going to win. It was just a matter of observing it happen.

The taxi from the airport kind of sticks in my mind. It ought to. Having loaded our bags into the boot, among the old fanbelts, wiper blades, tins of oil and other spare parts that Russians never throw away, we tied the lid down and started to run. The taxi had no first gear, so it couldn't get started with a full load on. But with a bit of a push, us running along until it got a bit of speed on, and then with a running jump, we managed to get on board and chugged off down the wide boulevard into Moscow.

Our hotel was a beauty. Called the Ukrainer, it looked like a gothic nightmare, designed in the days of Stalin, full of gargoyles and spires. It was huge and forbidding, and quite the worst hotel I have ever stayed in. After a long flight, I wanted to freshen up. But there was no shower. There was a bath, but it had no plug. Even if it had a plug, there was no hot water because this wasn't a hot water day. Hot water was only available twice a week, and today was not the day.

So, forgetting the wash, we gathered for dinner. The restaurant had just opened but there wasn't any food. It seems the staff simply passed it out the back door and sent it home to feed the relatives, leaving the guests with a decidedly slim menu of borscht and champagne. There was lots of champagne and, so the waiter told me, caviar. He told me it was cheap and dug into his deep pockets, fiddled around near his crotch and pulled out a small can, still warm and looking decidedly suspect. Rob and I drank champagne all night and, with empty stomachs, got thoroughly drunk. Welcome to Moscow.

Welcome also to the world of Natasha, Lydia, Raisa and Paulette.

As we made our way up to our rooms, past the elderly babushkas who guarded each floor and handed us our room keys, we couldn't help but notice the women who were waiting around, sitting in every available seat, leaning against the walls smoking cigarettes with what they must have thought were sultry poses, and flashing us the eye. They were there on every floor, and this was at least a ten-storey hotel.

The next morning, over coffee, those hookers were the hot topic. They had been ringing all the rooms in the wee small hours with a truly unique line of patter – "I love you, I love you and I want to come to your room." The old keepers of the keys had a heck of a sideline going, giving out names and room numbers to the hookers and no doubt being paid well for the information.

Strangely, they never rang me. As Phil, Chook and

The Final Burial of Communism

Rob described their calls (and denied any wrongdoing, of course) I could only wonder, why the hell didn't they call me? I really felt the odd one out, although they didn't believe me. Still, no time to sulk. I had a date with the Russian mafia.

Our interpreter, Paul Zhigalov, had told us to avoid the taxis. They were all run by the mafia and took foreigners for a ride. Although the meters would show 30 rubles, the drivers would simply add a nought on the end, give their company the 30 and share the excess 270 rubles with the mafia. For that the mafia kept the taxi ranks outside the hotels clear of any but their own drivers.

Paul had also told us that we could always flag down a passing motorist. The average Russian was desperate to earn foreign currency and was not above moonlighting in the taxi business. So I tried it, and the first person I waved at stopped. He was more than happy not to go to work that day and instead would be our driver around Moscow for as long as we wanted, and for a very reasonable rate.

The taxi drivers were irate. A number of them simply attacked our poor driver and no doubt threatened him with all sorts of Russian tortures. He drove away in a hurry, leaving us without a car. We had a job to do, places to go, and by now no choice. The mafia had won.

With the election in two days, the main event was to be a political rally that afternoon featuring Boris Yeltsin. He was already the president of the Russian republic but, like Russian leaders before him, he'd been appointed to the task. This election was all about giving people their chance to actually elect him for real, or someone else if they chose.

There was fat chance of that; even less after a massive show of support by some quarter of a million people who came to hear him speak. I couldn't understand a word he had to say but understood perfectly clearly that the crowd were behind him 99 per cent. Yeltsin was such a shoo-in he didn't even bother to appear for a final televised debate with his rivals.

Perhaps most telling were the Russian dolls on sale in Red Square; the traditional dolls inside the dolls. With Gorbachev still the Soviet leader, they were known as Gorby dolls. But on this day, even before the election had been held, a new version was on the streets. A tiny Lenin doll inside a Stalin doll, inside Khrushchev, inside Brezhnev, inside Gorbachev who was inside Yeltsin. The Gorby doll was dead, long live the Yeltsie.

There were other candidates, obviously not so popular as Yeltsin but quite interesting nevertheless. One was a raving lunatic by the name of Vladimir Zhirinovsky. His main election platform was cheap vodka for everyone. In a stunning piece of logic, he figured that the economic ills of Russia were so great he wouldn't even bother trying to fix them. He'd simply make vodka so cheap that everyone could afford to get drunk all the time and, in that way, forget their woes. What's more, Zhirinovsky spoke English. So off I went to find him.

It wasn't hard, and Zhirinovsky seemed delighted at the attention. He was a middle-sized man with blotchy skin and a florid complexion. What dominated his face were his faraway eyes. All he did was complain to us about the lies told about him, the falsifications and distortions. He suspected reds under every bed, although, given this was Moscow, that's hardly surprising. I concluded he was a raving monster loony, which is why I find it amazing that, just three years later, Russians elected this man to become a parliamentary leader and one of the most powerful men in the country. His subsequent embarrassment of Russia didn't surprise me a bit.

I concluded the day with some shopping in the magnificent GUM department store, Moscow's version of Harrod's or Bloomingdale's. Except GUM ain't no Harrod's. Just as in every other communist economy, there was nothing worth buying, unless plastic shoes, fur hats (in summer), enormous 1950s style bras, plastic mugs with Gorbachev's face on them or rubber boot liners were your thing. I can honestly say in an afternoon of looking I didn't find a single memento worth taking home.

The Moscow subway, though, was something else. It cost about half a cent to go anywhere. The trains were clean, fast and frequent. And the subway itself was breathtakingly beautiful, with magnificent frescos painted on all the walls and

The Final Burial of Communism

ceilings. It was nice to be impressed by something.

That night we weren't about to risk the hotel restaurant again. But we had been told about the "special" restaurants where, for US dollars, one could buy meals fit for a king (they had to be, at the prices they charged). Perhaps the restaurant our taxi driver took us to that night might not impress people much these days. But in Moscow, at that time, it was something out of this world. The plates weren't chipped, the cutlery was clean and matching, the wine was French, the food was edible; it's just the one hundred US dollars a main course that made the food a little unpalatable.

Back to our hotel to run the gauntlet of those hookers and back to my room to find the one and only working light bulb in my room had disappeared, along with my soap and shaving cream. But I had been warned that this country, with nuclear weapons and men in space, had trouble supplying the most basic of necessities.

Election day was a curious affair, largely devoid of the colour and emotion one could reasonably have expected. After all the places and events I'd been to over the previous couple of years, I was well placed to judge. Perhaps it was the predictability of Yeltsin's victory? He won nearly three-quarters of the vote, and that was clear before the day was out. Russians seemed weary, which I found surprising given the history that was being made this day.

I made a point of seeking out the oldest voter I could find. I stopped an elderly woman as she entered the voting booth and, through an interpreter, asked her age. She was around 85; born before the revolution. She had lived through the rise and fall of communism and would die a free woman. Relatively free. And so democracy came to Russia on the 13th of June, 1991.

We celebrated the historic occasion with dinner back at the hotel, although celebration is a bit of an exaggeration. It was a hot water night in our hotel. We clogged one of our baths with toilet paper (unique stuff that didn't break down no matter how wet it got), filled it with hot water and broke out the emergency rations we'd been advised to bring. Ready-made lasagnas from Marks and Spencers; just heat and eat.

If it's hard getting into Russia, then it's even harder getting out. The lady at customs was straight out of a bad novel – large, imposing, hair tied back in a strict bun, intimidating uniform and a very aggressive manner. When film crews move in and out of countries with equipment worth hundreds of thousands of dollars, we have to clear customs using forms called carnets. On those forms, every single serial number of every single piece of equipment is recorded.

I have never been asked to check them off against each other – it is simply too big and time-consuming a task. But this customs official seemed determined to do just that, even if it meant us missing our plane. As she started her search, a commotion broke out nearby.

It seems customs was having a problem with a Vietnamese traveller. He'd broken away from the men escorting him, made a rush for a large group of fellow Vietnamese standing behind us, then thrown his briefcase over our heads. It fell to the floor and broke open to reveal wads of money. The Vietnamese fell upon the money and frantically tried to pick it up, while Russian security guards fell upon the Vietnamese. A right royal melee ensued.

The offender then decided to try to get away and came running at us. Without really thinking, Rob and I grabbed him as he tried to get by and held him for just a few seconds until two airport officials grabbed him and took him away to a small room off the side of the concourse. Before they'd even closed the door they'd begun hitting him around the head.

As for us? Our customs clearance was immediate. All of a sudden it was all smiles, no need to check the numbers, dasvidanya and goodnight.

That should have been it, except it was up to me to pay the huge excess baggage bill. The others went through passport control while I went to take care of business. The excess baggage office was off to one side, and I lined up to wait. Soon I was joined by a large group of very short Vietnamese who started to push and crowd me, trying to get to the front of the line.

The Final Burial of Communism

I'm used to the European concept of personal space; they were used to the Vietnamese concept of no personal space. As they pressed up against me on all sides, I began to feel decidedly uncomfortable. When one little chap got down on hands and knees, crawled between my legs and stood up between me and the counter I just lost it. I cannot recall ever losing my temper in public like this before. I just grabbed the intruder and threw him out of the way, spun round and growled at the others in a universal language to stand back and give me some room, and turned to do my business. There was stunned silence for all of one point five seconds, then the pushing and shoving began again.

I should not have been surprised when the officials began demanding cash for the excess baggage. I certainly didn't have a thousand dollars US on me and, more to the point, I knew they only wanted it for their own purposes. They would pay the bill in rubles, pocket the dollars and make a huge profit. The argument dragged on as I refused to pay cash and they refused to accept any of my credit cards. It was a standoff, and all the while the time was ticking away, while the crowd behind me grew angrier and angrier. Finally they blinked, seized my Amex card and angrily processed the claim. Detente was preserved.

In time, I made the plane and we took off. It used to be customary for Western travellers to applaud as their aircraft lifts off from Moscow. I clapped particularly loudly.

The October Coup

Cameron Bennett

From Moscow, CNN is live with the story – there's a coup under way against Boris Yeltsin's stumbling new democracy. It's October 1993 and I am in Swansea, Wales, previewing the Kiwi rugby league squad. While our boys are kicking a ball around a paddock, potentially catastrophic history is in the making as the new Russia teeters in the balance.

Twenty-four hours later, I am standing in front of the blazing Russian parliament, known as the White House, delivering a piece-to-camera about the day's dramatic events.

That's the way the job was. You never knew from one day to the next what you'd be covering. In the four weeks leading up to Moscow, I'd been to Bosnia, covered an open-air concert by Kiri Te Kanawa in Bath, reported on the world chess championships and a Kiwi fashion store in London, been up to Northampton to profile driving ace Paul Radisich, filmed in Antwerp, covered the start of the Whitbread yacht race in Southampton, been across to Dublin for a feature on golden oldie rugby players and travelled to Wales for the rugby league.

There was barely time to catch your breath, or change your mind-set from the business of strained ligaments and tackling form to the serious issues of international affairs.

Foreign Correspondents

The October coup was no different. It had been weeks in the coming. Yeltsin, his policies sabotaged by an unsympathetic parliament, had taken matters into his own hands. He simply dissolved the assembly and brought tanks onto the streets to deal with the resistance. Then came the state of emergency, street rallies were banned, opposition parties were suspended – including the founding party of the communist state – and tough new censorship laws imposed on all but a few loyal newspapers.

Opposition leaders – principally Speaker Ruslan Khasbalatov and Yeltsin's deputy Alexander Rhutskoi – were holed up in the Russian parliament. A fortnight-long standoff had finally flared into violence on October 3.

From our offices in Isleworth, Middlesex, we watched and waited along with the world. When the first shell was fired at the White House by tanks loyal to Yeltsin, it was our signal to go.

A hectic catch-up followed. Hugh Riminton from Channel 9, Mark Llewellyn from *A Current Affair*, myself, cameraman Peter Watts and sound recordist/editor Brendan Donohoe left London with tickets for Alaska, scheduled for a stop-over in Moscow. We had no time to apply for visas, and anyway, that could have taken up to a fortnight. Our story was well-rehearsed for the Russian officials: we were en route to an environmental conference in the United States.

Arriving at Moscow's dingy airport, we nervously made our way down to the customs officers. They refused to stamp our passports. We would have to wait our turn and discuss visas with a more senior official. We knew our ruse could work. Other journalists had bluffed their way in. Nevertheless, there was still the very good risk that we would not be let out of the airport, given the unrest. Because of our ongoing tickets to Alaska, we'd made sure not to bring anything other than hand luggage to avoid complications. As it turned out, the senior official needed little convincing of our intentions. All he wanted was $US100 per visa and we were in.

So, there we were standing in the cold outside Moscow airport with not a word of Russian between us. It was running close to curfew hour – we had little time to make it to a hotel, let alone shoot piece-to-cameras. We bundled into a Volga taxi with a driver whose English extended to such words as "Radisson Hotel" and "Kremlin", and ground our way into town. The driver was edgy – not just about the curfew but also over the stray gunfire. Volleys of machinegun and semi-automatic fire were still reverberating round the capital.

With just minutes before the curfew came into effect we found the vantage point for our piece-to-cameras, the flaming White House in the background. Halfway round the world, TVNZ foreign editor Mark Boyd and his team were processing the reports that had flowed in while we were still in the air. That information would form the bulk of my report. By 5am I was huddled in my cameraman's hotel room, voicing my script direct into the camera. That voice-over and my piece-to-camera would be played down the satellite link to New Zealand, the team in Auckland "colouring it in" with syndicated pictures. It was dramatic stuff, *One Network News* running with some four and a half minutes in the lead slot. More than 170 people had been killed, 900 wounded and almost 1300 arrested.

Brendan Donohoe suffered his own dramas that night. He'd been forced to share his room with our taxi driver, who had been unable to go home because of the curfew. The driver spent the night watching pornography on satellite TV and drinking the mini bar dry. If that wasn't enough, he scuttled off at first light, leaving us without a driver to take us to the satellite playout facility.

It was exhilarating to again be covering the world's number one story. I began my career as an inept cadet reporter on the *Northern Advocate* in Whangarei, and I never failed to pinch myself in situations like Moscow, to remind myself that I'd come a long way since then. There is a tremendous thrill and sense of having "made it" as a reporter when you are signing off your report from international hotspots ". . . Cameron Bennett, *One Network News*, Moscow."

The journalism is one thing, the logistics quite another. When a reporter or presenter appears on your television screen there can be no knowing what went on behind the screens to get them there – and nor should there be.

In the field in Europe for TVNZ there is no on-the-ground back-up. You are it, you have to make it happen: arranging and hiring editing time, ensuring there are satellite "windows" available to transmit your reports, arranging transport, visas, foreign currency, negotiating hired cars around cities you have never seen before, coping with language barriers. All that before you can even think about journalism – a far cry from the Auckland newsroom and its support systems.

For me, "live-shots" were generally the most fraught because they seemed to be required in the most awkward of situations. The live-shot usually consisted of what's known in the trade as a "doughnut": a lead-in statement at the top of the report and then coming off the back with another statement, and then some question-and-answer from the show hosts.

In the chaos of Moscow it was little short of a nightmare. Most of the foreign broadcasters' satellite dishes were on top of the White House and had been incinerated along with half a dozen of the building's upper floors. Temporary dishes were hastily set up; we were booked with Worldwide Television News. Frantic efforts to establish audio and stable vision between Auckland and Europe were not unusual, the problems often only being sorted out seconds before on-air time. But this was in a league of its own. Nothing was operating normally, not least the audio links. Instead of the usual sound-mix box and earpiece to allow me a clear line to TVNZ, I was standing with a telephone receiver taped to my back and a plastic tube running to my ear. Sound came and went and in the frantic minutes before on-air time I was dashing up and down two flights of stairs from the feedpoint to a telephone in the WTN office. We managed to patch a satellite call via New York. Another sprint up the stairs and back in front of the live camera. I could hear Richard Long's questions, but only just, through the echo and time delay. In circumstances like that you just box on regardless and hope you haven't cut off the question.

To see that charred White House in the days after Yeltsin had restored control, to feel the eerie sense of uncertainty in the city which ruled over an empire I had grown up as fearing most, was an unsettling experience.

I had been here before, almost seven months earlier on tour with Prime Minister Jim Bolger. The purpose of the trip was largely to ensure that old Soviet debts to New Zealand producer boards could be repaid. By being part of the prime ministerial entourage, I was able to tour inside the Kremlin itself. To walk the corridors that had been trod by Stalin, Khrushchev, Brezhnev, Gorbachev, the Tsars . . . there was an inescapable sense of history.

We were there too when Bolger met Yeltsin, the Russian President entering the room with a waxy complexion and stiff of gait as though his neck and spine were fused. We'd also met his ebullient vice-president, Alexander Rhutskoi – the flamboyant hero of the Afghani campaign all flowing moustache and confidence. He had visited New Zealand in his official capacity. Now he and his fellow plotters were locked up in Moscow's infamous Lefortovo Prison. Amidst the barrage on the White House his desperate pleas for police units to defect to his cause had gone unheeded. Khasbalatov – the Speaker of the House who had been under intense media spotlight as the crisis built – reportedly chain-smoked his pipe while slumped in an armchair, muttering to nobody in particular, "I have known Yeltsin for a long time, but I never expected anything like this from him."

Moscow seemed like a scruffy, sprawling contradiction. How could such a shabby, broken-down town have managed to have struck such terror in the West for so long? Even Red Square seemed diminished. Red Square, where every year we watched news clips of the annual parade of Soviet military hardware rumble past the party leadership on the Kremlin walls, had the aura of something vast. In fact, it is much smaller than it looks on those TV clips. St Basil's Cathedral, too, at the far end, with its gaudy swirls and onion-like twists, is little more than an incomplete shell. The only

real symbol of communist might left, it appeared that
tumultuous October, was the goose-stepping guard of honour
which had paraded round-the-clock outside Lenin's tomb
since the founder of the communist state was buried there in
1924. But even that would go. I was in Red Square for the final
parade by that precision guard. Yeltsin, in a last gesture of
contempt for his communist enemies, had already signed the
order for the eternal honour guard to be disbanded.

The contradictions abound at all levels. For instance,
the best bars to drink at are Irish bars. Not only that, Moscow
boasts a quality of Guinness that you'd be hard-pressed to find
outside of Dublin. Why Irish bars? It apparently started with a
concession to an Irish company to open a pub at Moscow
airport, and grew from there. Drinking remains the only true
solace in Moscow. Foreigners drink Guinness, Muscovites
drink vodka, despite Gorbachev's best efforts to limit its flow.
Muscovites fall over drunk and so do foreigners. I was witness
to the fact. At the end of my first visit to the Russian capital, I'd
been invited to an Irish bar which was a hot favourite with
journos and expat businessmen. I spent the evening with a no-
concessions Aussie crew based in Moscow. After a full night's
refreshments they drove me back to my hotel. And, in a show
of bravado that would impress even the most seasoned
Muscovite bon vivant, the sound recordist, a woman, threw up
on the doorman's polished boots as he opened the car door.

On the streets, the local militia survives on a pitiful
wage. They will flag you down on the road and demand a spot
fine – in cash – for no other reason than to supplement their
income. The air of corruption is all around; impoverished
militiamen watching immensely wealthy gangsters parading
down the prospekt in BMWs and Porsches. The hotel lobbies
are prime locations for Moscow's enormous trade in
prostitution.

Money talks in this town, although there are few
Western-style shopping complexes. Women stand on street
corners holding up items for sale, women from all walks of life.
Container sheds are set up on footpaths as makeshift stalls.
But the ultimate market-place had to be the endless stalls of

The October Coup

the Arbat. Here, on my first visit in March 1993, you could buy virtually any piece of military hardware you wanted.

There's something depressing about peering in on the degradation of a society; particularly this one, which had been forged out of such tragedy and deprivation. In Moscow, it was in the air – a sense of uncertainty. Almost as if, with their belief-structures gone, the apparent invincibility of Soviet power gone, ordinary Muscovites had been left with nothing other than their crumbling civic facilities and turmoil. That loss of dignity and identity, I discovered, is a shared experience in the old communist bloc countries. That and a shared sense of resentment. My first taste of that passion came in Dresden, part of the old East Germany, while filming a commemorative feature on the effects of Allied bombing in wartime. A debate had emerged on Sir Arthur ("Bomber") Harris and whether he deserved to be honoured for his relentless attacks on civilian targets. It was February 1992 and a group of young intellectuals in Dresden, who'd been part of the revolution to overthrow communism, were reflecting on the effects of Western democracy and capitalism on their country. They observed that, ". . . though there was so very much wrong with our system, there were some things that perhaps you Westerners could learn. We had a system that cared for people . . . we cherished values such as debate and music above money . . ."

After reporting on those giddy October days, my job was done. It seemed a good few Westerners were leaving about the same time. Those of us booked on Aeroflot hastily changed to British Airways. After interminable delays we set off for London. The drinks trolley had barely made its way into the cabin before the party started. Everyone, it seemed, was of the same mind – delighted to be out of there. The party lasted the entire journey, no-one sitting it out, including a familiar face a few seats back, the actor John Hurt.

Baptism of Fire

Cameron Bennett

War became real for me in July 1992. In the seven days cameraman Richard Malone and I spent in Sarajevo, we would know for the first time the terror of being targeted by snipers, we would be exposed for the first time to the pain of civilian casualties, the heart-wrenching funerals of the war dead, the hopeless desolation of refugees. I would experience for the first time the strange cocktail of emotions that are part of being a witness to war. I was there to share the dread that shuddered through the press corps after a bullet smashed through the window of a CNN van, ripping off the lower half of fellow Kiwi Margaret Moth's face. I had been talking to her shortly before it happened.

I made three tours of Bosnia between 1992 and '95. But, in many ways, it is that first tour which remains the most vivid for me. It's difficult to communicate how inexperienced I was for such an assignment. In preparing for it, I was on my own. There was no-one I knew who'd reported a war like this. Journalists covering the Gulf War were not allowed anywhere near the front line; Bosnia was a different situation altogether. Here there were no front lines. This was no conventional war – it was highly unpredictable civil war. Here journalists could not rely on the discipline and protection of regular army units as they would in, say, the Gulf. For reporters like myself it would turn out to be a case of every man for himself. There would be no support system or protection from the United Nations troops and their tanks. It was just you, your crew, your map and your car and away you go.

To give some perspective to the dangers of covering the Yugoslav conflict, in the year leading up to my arrival there in 1992, at least 30 reporters, photographers and cameramen had lost their lives or were missing, presumed dead. In just 12 months the death toll was fast approaching the total of newsmen killed during the 15 years of conflict in Vietnam.

The reason for me taking the risk of adding to the body count was the Kiwi angle. Some eight New Zealand military observers were based in the splintered remains of Yugoslavia at the time. One of them, Major John Bryant, was lying in a hospital in Zagreb, Croatia, nursing injuries received when his jeep drove over a land-mine. He was my first story. More observers were posted in the Bosnian capital of Sarajevo. Both my news executives in Auckland and myself believed that by featuring New Zealanders in our reports, coupled with my own impressions, we would be able to provide a context to this war that viewers back home could relate to.

Richard Malone had come fresh from an assignment on competition swimmers in Spain and arrived complete with an underwater housing for his camera. Using his very best colloquial "Ocker", he dined out on that to the hilarity of the press corps. Richard also did his best to look like he'd arrived fresh from Bondi Beach, choosing board shorts and a surfing tee-shirt over the regulation media fatigues and fishing jacket. Richard is a laid-back Tasmanian, who is remembered by anyone who works with him for his remarkable vagueness and his remarkable talent with the lens. There's a very special friendship and respect you develop for a colleague who is prepared to go through the sort of privations and dangers we did on that tour. I can't think of a greater test of character, grit and sense of humour in a man. Bosnia is a baptism of fire.

Baptism of Fire

We couldn't have come much greener, though. Our flak jackets were a couple of woefully inadequate hand-me-downs from the Gulf War. Apart from helping look the part, they would have done nothing to stop a sniper's bullet. The other media people were decked out in jackets with keflar plates front and back. Some even sported protective cod-pieces. From day one I could see we were badly under-dressed, but that was the least of it. I had no provision for war insurance or danger money. Both are standard outlays on war correspondents, as I would later discover. Maps of Sarajevo had been unavailable in Zagreb, so I didn't have one of those either. In short, there was no choice but to "wing it", and that's exactly what I did.

Our only option for travelling in was to fly. It took us two days to secure places on board an Italian Hercules. Of the five of us, perched on the webbing seats as we roared through Croatian airspace, none had been in before. We masked our nervousness with wisecracks but the closer we got to Sarajevo, the quieter we all became. We were immersed in our own thoughts. Mine were with my wife Phyl and sons Angus and Calum back in London. What if I'm injured or killed? Why am I doing this? Why am I putting my family through this? I was deeply worried, too, about Richard. He also had a wife back in London. I felt a heavy sense of responsibility for his safety. But just as the Hercules plunged down towards Sarajevo airport, he shouted over the engine noise: "Mate, if I'm hit I'm not about to blame you."

Sarajevo airport was like none other that I had been to. The terminal was sandbagged and shot-up. United Nations machinegun posts were set up at regular intervals. Nobody walked on the tarmac unless they had to – it was just too dangerous. There was no customs clearance. But more alarming for us, there was no transport out. Luckily, we ran into another Kiwi and a veteran of the conflict. Simon Townsley was a photographer for the British *Sunday Times*; he also had a car.

At that time, the media did not have armoured cars. They had either bought, at extortionate prices, a local car or had driven their own vehicles in. VW Golfs, Audis and Vauxhalls were uniformly scraped and dented or had lost their windows to gunfire. Simon's car was no different.

The stretch of road from the airport to the UN headquarters and then on into the city is about as perilous as it gets. It starts the moment you clear the airport gates. Your adrenalin pumps uncontrollably. Every vehicle is a potential target for snipers holed up in the pocked and abandoned buildings just a few hundred metres away. You drive at breakneck speed, and if there are any windows left in the car, you wind them down. Otherwise, there's the danger of flying glass if the car takes a direct hit. Another "no" was to sit in the back of a two-door car. The simple reason for that was the difficulty of getting out in a hurry. It was also suggested that journalists driving non-armoured cars should leave the doors ajar so they could dive out easily.

No sooner had we set off, ducking and weaving around a UN armoured convoy, than the crackle of gunfire started up. I was too new to it all to associate the shooting with our car. It all seemed too unreal. Simon put me right on that count. On almost every car ride we took after that we were shot at by someone sitting with a sniper's gun in an empty warehouse or apartment.

One of the closest shaves was at the airport a few days later. We'd hitched a lift with other journalists back out along the stretch known as "murder mile", from the UN headquarters on Marshal Tito Boulevard to the airport. A Greek television journalist had told me there was a car out there that we could hire. At the time, anything seemed better than hitching lifts and walking, which is what we were doing. No sooner had we got out of our car than a bullet slammed into an iron railing just metres away from us. Without hesitation, we sprinted for cover. And as for the hire car, it turned out to be undriveable. A South African cameraman, Brian Green – a man I'd meet again in Bosnia and in Africa – "hotwired" it for us but the steering had been damaged. The car would only drive in a circle. So, we'd again risked our lives, and this time for a car that didn't even work.

Baptism of Fire

It seems incredible, but you can rapidly become complacent in a place like Sarajevo. Not when you are caught up in a fire-fight or mortar exchange; the danger then is obvious and you take cover. But it is on those otherwise quiet afternoons when people are walking about freely and you are tempted to do the same without your hot and heavy flak jacket. It's then that you are at your most vulnerable, because the sniper shots, when they come, are like bolts from the blue. The good shooters rarely miss. A year later I would learn that first-hand after meeting one who had accounted for 27 lives.

Neven Luledzija was a most unlikely-looking killer. He had a soft, smiling, bearded face. He wore his hair long and he wore glasses. He walked with a pronounced limp. We happened upon him while filming streetscapes in old Sarajevo. He approached us looking for work. He spoke excellent English so I hired him. Neven had been a radio producer before the war, he was also an excellent shot with a sports rifle. That was how he ended up a sniper for the Bosnian Presidency forces. At the time, a sniper was supported by two "watchers" who selected the prey. The targets were not civilians then, they were the opposition.

I remember interviewing Neven one sultry afternoon about his experiences. I was suffering badly from a fatigue-induced headache, but what he had to say was too compelling not to concentrate. He told of the more than two dozen men he'd killed as a sniper and how clearly he'd been able to see each of their faces through his telescopic sights. I asked him whether he now suffered from a guilty conscience and war neurosis. He said, "If you mean, do I wake up sweating and screaming at night when those faces return to me . . . yes I suffer war neurosis."

There was a weary fatalism about Neven – he was just waiting his turn. One quiet afternoon, while filming from our car the scarred buildings and abandoned trams along Marshal Tito Boulevard, an artillery shell lobbed in less than 30 metres from us. Luckily, much of the fallout was absorbed by a low wall. We had obviously been the target. From the back seat of the car Neven impassively announced that it was a howitzer shell and that we would be wise to move. I got our car out of there as fast as I could.

I had planned for us to stay at the Holiday Inn Hotel. But, without transport, I could not guarantee that we could get to and from the television building to edit and satellite out my reports. Instead I opted to hire an office in the concrete monolith that is the Bosnian television station. It had taken many direct hits, but there were few buildings safer.

There was no choice but to sleep on the floor; there were no beds. At night we were forced to crawl on all fours out of sight of the window because of the snipers, while by day we made sure never to stand in front of it either. There were no showers and the toilets were rancid and clogged from over-use. It was under these circumstances that I learnt the value of dry shampoo. It's a powdery, talcum-like spray that can make even the greasiest locks look passable in front of a television camera. Food was another problem, because the staff canteen at the time could only offer small quantities of bread and an unremitting diet of watery soup. In fact, the only real difference between the soup and a bowl of hot water were the blobs of fat floating on the surface.

Looking back on it now, it seems we lived more on adrenalin, Marlboro cigarettes and doses of slivovice – the local firewater – than food. Day and night rolled into one. In the daylight hours, we compressed in a remarkable array of experiences; by night we edited them into news and feature packages. A week felt like a year. We were exhausted by lack of sleep and the relentless pressure of working in a war zone.

Filing my first report out of Sarajevo was an experience I'll remember for the rest of my life. Lying on our office floor, my cameraman and I woke up that morning to the roar of mortar and artillery fire exploding between the TV station and the UN headquarters, which is where we were due to satellite out our story at the BBC's play-out facility. We had only one way of getting there – on foot. Whether we should try it or not was an agonising decision. After monitoring a lull in the explosions, I decided we had a good chance, but insisted that Richard did not have to come. He decided he would, so off we set down a notorious stretch of road nicknamed by journalists as "Snipers' Alley".

In its survival guide, the Committee to Protect Journalists advises against wearing military-style clothes. Great. About the only thing going for our flimsy flak jackets was their thoroughly military appearance. I wore a cotton sports jacket over the top of mine hoping that any militiaman up in the hills would not confuse me with a combatant. Minutes after setting off for the UN building, the mortar fire started up again. Our clothes meant nothing now and we sprinted for our lives, arriving breathless and bathed in sweat at the UN building and with little time to spare before satellite deadline.

"You take the tape down to the BBC and I'll get set up for the live-shot," I told Richard. He stared at me with a look of horror. "Haven't you got it?" We both realised in absolute despair that, in the excitement of it all, we had forgotten to bring the edited beta-tape of my report.

The moments afterwards were blurred by panic. How could I salvage the situation? We couldn't possibly run back for it. Apart from the danger, we'd be too late for the deadline. Luckily, at the time, a colourful New Zealander by the name of Colonel Richard Gray was holding down a senior position at the UN. I pleaded our case and he broke all the rules by ordering a driver to take me back to the TV station to collect the tape. I've seldom felt more grateful.

There were others, too, who were crucial to our success. One was a thin and traumatised Serbian woman who lived at the TV station. Olga Pantelenac, fresh from film school, had come to Sarajevo from Belgrade shortly before the war. A few months later Yugoslavia broke apart and she was left stranded. She deeply opposed the aggression of her own country, but equally did not want to remain in Bosnia for the war. Without a passport and documents she had no other choice. Olga helped edit my reports late at night when Richard was just too dog-tired to cut them himself. She is a delicate, refined woman. When I knew her she was a nervous wreck. At the height of the bombardment of Sarajevo, she'd spent days alone in a burnt-out basement with the carcass of a dead cat. At the TV station, she worked for no pay – just the right to exist in safety. She chain-smoked. She would come and smoke and drink with us in our little office in the early hours of the morning after the editing was complete.

Like Melisa Tolja, who I would meet a year later, she triggered a desperate longing in us to want to help. We organised Simon Townsley to shoot passport pictures of her. Other foreign journalists were later able to organise her a place on a flight to Croatia. But Croatia was no place for a refugee Serb, she needed to travel to neighbouring Slovenia. But the Slovenes wouldn't take her unless she could guarantee an ongoing destination. I helped organise that by faxing the British embassy in Zagreb with a guarantee of sponsorship for her to visit us in Britain. It was enough to get her a visa for Slovenia, where she resides today.

Mirko ("Miki") Kurilic came into my life one morning at the UN building. One of two Bosnian police liaison officers working there, he was another caught up in the trap that was Sarajevo. A Bosnian Serb and the son of a distinguished army officer, he'd had the foresight to evacuate his Muslim wife and child, but he'd stayed. When I met him he desperately needed money and was willing to drive us and act as my interpreter.

Miki was our ticket into the "human" story of Sarajevo. He would drive us, like a lunatic, down the deadly "Snipers' Alley". One section of it was particularly dangerous; a cross-roads that frequently became a shooting gallery. There you hurtled through a chicane of obstacles, foot flat to the floor. The *crack crack crack* was all the confirmation you needed that you were in the snipers' sights. On one occasion, we caught that drama on film as the shots cracked in close to our car. "Snipers' Alley" does not have a specific beginning or end. Virtually any intersection or section of road visible from the hills forms an extended snipers' alley. Any car was a target for the marksmen and as there were so few of them on the road at the time – and because journalists drove most of those that were – there was the good chance that any "kills" would be foreign newsmen.

Baptism of Fire

Miki introduced us to the poorly resourced Kosevo Hospital and to the battered back-streets of the old town. It was there I met a black African toting an AK-47. I asked him what an African was doing fighting for the Bosnian government. He shrugged his shoulders and said he'd been a student here when the war began and he had no other choice. I met one soldier who wore a cowboy hat and had two pearl-handled silver Colts.

I saw breathtakingly attractive women in their fashionable clothes sipping fake coffee in cafes, as if there was no war going on at all. I watched kids playing war with wooden guns. I watched a young woman, overwrought with grief, running her fingers through the soil of her husband's freshly dug grave. I saw an old man weep when Richard gave him a couple of cigarettes. I drank brandy at nine in the morning with an import-exporter who could no longer import or export. I saw the veteran BBC reporter Martin Bell and his crew arrive back after their Vauxhall Cavalier had collected two or maybe more direct hits to one of the door pillars. I watched Margaret Moth's producer (he'd been sitting just in front of her when she was hit) remove one of her teeth from his bloodied sweatshirt as he frantically prepared for a live cross to CNN. We didn't know if she would live or not.

I was badly shaken by that incident. A fellow New Zealander – it could have been me. The bullet just missed a key artery but blew away most of her jaw, shattering cheek bones and severing her tongue. I will never forget our own farewell dash to the airport a day or so later. Richard and I hunched in the back of a battered "soft-skin" Audi as it hurtled first through the Muslim checkpoint and on to the flyover that takes you to the airport road. I've rarely felt so frightened. There was an ominous sense that this was going to be our turn. "On the trip out, that's when they'll get you," I thought. "That's when they got John McCarthy."

I returned to Sarajevo in August 1993, this time driving in from the Croatian coastal city of Split with my old mate Richard Malone on camera and Brendan Donohoe as sound recordist and tape editor. The car was an Opel Senator, a former German diplomatic vehicle. Its windows were six centimetres thick.

There were two Senators to choose from; we chose the one with the sweetest-sounding motor. The downside was that its windows were weakened by gunshots. Jim Nachtwey, the famous *Time* photographer, chose the other. We met him later in Sarajevo. He told us how the car had broken down in the furious battleground of Gorni Vakuf, in central Bosnia. Not only that, he'd been mortared as a British tank came to tow him out. "A serious pain in the ass," was how he described it. Not the mortaring, but the fact that he'd been delayed for his assignment. I would see Nachtwey again on assignment in South Africa and in Rwanda where one of his photos won him the World Press Photo of the Year in 1994.

Again, for me, this was new and dangerous territory. I had not been overland before. The plan was to travel with a UN convoy from Split to Tomislavgrad and over the so-called "Triangle" route into central Bosnia. It didn't turn out that way. The UN convoy was delayed indefinitely. We would have to go alone, but not before some soul-searching. Brendan – who proved to be another exceptional man in my experience – wanted to know how safe the journey would be. What could I say? I didn't know. We could only go on the experience of other crews who'd made it through safely. We decided to take our chances, setting off in a car loaded down with jerry cans of petrol, food, water and camera equipment.

The car overheated on the steep, gravelled roads of the Triangle. I wanted to reach the safety of British Battalion HQ in Vitez before nightfall. Given the problems of the heavily-laden car on the tortuous roads, we knew the chances were slim, but not before overshooting the frontline Croatian garrison town of Prozor and driving straight into highly dangerous Gorni Vakuf. I was behind the wheel. Realising our mistake I spun the car around back to Prozor about the same time as a couple of shots came our way.

Prozor is no place for a foreign journalist. Drunken soldiers lurk menacingly on the streets while others wildly career around in cars. It is Wild West. There are few civilians

Baptism of Fire

and nothing in the way of hotels. I managed, through a local commander, to negotiate beds in an army-requisitioned flat, discovering later that, having given you a bed for the night, the soldiers steal your car. Why they didn't with us, I still don't know.

Driving alone in the central Bosnia of 1993 was a fraught business. The changing front lines were like zebra stripes on a map. You could cross from one to another some times with barely a kilometre in between. You'd be stopped at road blocks, not knowing which army the soldiers belonged to.

The Committee to Protect Journalists' handbook advises at times like this to "Schmooze. Troops at checkpoints might be drunk, pumped with adrenalin or otherwise socially impaired. Act like a buddy. If they detain you, seek allies among your captors."

We used Marlboro cigarettes to "schmooze". They worked most of the time, but not always. On the journey back up central Bosnia we had made our way to the Zenica-Vitez junction. Vitez is the base for the British battalion. We'd had an uneventful trip north and were looking to top our fuel at Britbat. I was driving, as I did on both my journeys overland to Sarajevo, partly because of a sense of responsibility for the vehicle but mostly because of the crew I'd brought in with me. The sense of responsibility for their lives – even though they didn't demand that – weighed heavily on me.

I still don't know how it happened, but militiamen directed us along a different route from that we'd taken out of Vitez a week earlier. With no guide or interpreter, we presumed the main route was too dangerous. Instead we were directed through a nearby village. The locals were out and about; it looked untroubled. But the scene changed for us within a matter of just a few hundred metres. We approached a stretch of road that was deathly quiet. The houses on either side were war-damaged and unoccupied. It didn't feel right but before we had time to change our minds, gunfire opened up all around us. Where were the shots coming from? We could only guess. We were terrified. I put the car into a three-point turn.

Foreign Correspondents

Richard was shouting "Watch out for the ditch . . ." I made the turn. Incredibly, we had still not been hit. Brendan was lying as flat as he could on the back seat.

It's extremely difficult to think clearly when bullets are cracking and whining around you. The report of a rifle is much louder than the muffled bangs I was used to on television. You don't know which way to turn. Your senses are confused – are they shooting from this direction or that direction? Hesitation would kill us, I knew that. I bottomed the accelerator, praying the car wouldn't stall. But it felt like we were barely moving. Then, out of the corner of my eye, a figure with a machinegun or semi-automatic loomed out of window just metres away. He opened up over the top of us. *Bam bam bam bam bam* in rapid fire. The noise was deafening. I had my neck hunched as far as it would go into my flak jacket, just waiting for the bullets to shatter our reinforced glass. They never came. And then it was over – we were through. Within a matter of seconds we were back on those apparently untroubled streets we'd just left. Later, and still fluttery from shock, we shared cigarettes at a European Commission post. A commander there informed us that an aid convoy driver had been killed on that same road a week earlier. His reinforced cabin was punctured by an armour-piercing bullet.

There is a stretch of exposed land that runs from near Santici (where Kiwi Company would eventually be based) and Vitez. On the hills above it were a series of redoubts. From those redoubts, anyone travelling the road below was fair game. We'd been potted at in Vitez on the journey in – once while Brendan was relieving himself by the roadside. Now, after the terrifying shoot-out in the nearby village, we were set to run the gauntlet again.

With helmets and flak jackets buckled and the car blaring out Deep Purple's *Smoke on the Water*, I gunned the car as fast as it would go. Near Vitez itself a roadblock made out of tank-traps appeared from nowhere. It hadn't been there on the way in. Men armed with semi-automatics ran towards us in crouched positions. I remember seeing the lumpy round shapes of Claymore-style mines on either side of the road. At gunpoint we were ordered off the road and down a track. We were terrified. Who were they – BIH (Bosnian army) or Croatian? What did they want? Money? The car? Are they planning to shoot us? They were clearly nervous, darting glances over their shoulders at the nearby hills. We were all in range of snipers. Incredibly, it seemed to be over as quickly as it started. They checked our UN accreditation then ran off in the same half-crouched way they'd approached us. What a moment. The only way back to the road was to reverse up the track. My heart was thumping. Are there mines on either side of the track? If I misjudge it we could be blown up. And what about the snipers?

We fuelled up in Vitez and headed for the Triangle and relative safety – or so we thought. Bandits rather than fighting units were now the biggest threat to an unescorted car. Our final drama came on the outskirts of Prozor. Up ahead was a Croatian militia bus. For all the world it looked like a post-match rugby supporters' bus; beers cans hurtling out the window as it wove its way up the hill. These were soldiers returning from the front line. As I pulled up behind, waiting for an opportunity to overtake, one drunken hoon hung out the back door and started taking pot shots with a pistol. I moved out of range only to notice that by favouring the other side of the bus we were now the target of another soldier who had pushed his semi-automatic rifle out a window and was pointing it in our direction. He emptied off a magazine but his aim was too wild. By that point we were past caring. I overtook them at the first opportunity and then drove for broke, non-stop back to Split. We left the bar that night barely able to stand.

I had never expected to live life quite so on the edge. I have never been a thrill-seeker. Rollercoasters make me feel ill and, even as a kid, I never sought out those activities that left you with an adrenalin high. Yet here I was in the middle of one of the most deadly wars journalists have covered in recent times, and in the company of some of the most outrageous journalists I have ever met.

In Sarajevo, the Holiday Inn was where most of them

stayed. It is a Hotel from Hell. Virtually no part of the building is safe and no window intact. It is steadily targeted from the surrounding hills by marksmen and artillery batteries. One whole section of it is in ruins. Power and water are intermittent at best. It is the only hotel I've heard of where people wear their flak jackets inside! You never stand exposed by an open door or leave by the front entrance. That's how the hotel gardener was shot.

During my first stay, my bedroom was up on the 10th floor. Getting there meant clambering up the stairs as the lift did not work. The longer you stayed, the better your chances of a room on the much sought after first or second floors. The glass had long before been shot out of the window. In its place was a sheet of opaque plastic. The toilet didn't flush because there was no running water. Each morning, staff would leave two wine bottles filled with fresh water outside my door – my ration for the day. The lights didn't work either, because there was no power. My penlight was the only available light. I made sure to stay well away from its glow, and to negotiate my way around the room on hands and knees because of the snipers. Exhaustion guaranteed a good night's sleep, even though the evening was punctuated by the steady clatter of machinegun and small arms fire. Tracer bullets and flares would light up the night sky.

The Holiday Inn was peopled by an odd assortment of guests. There were the "Rambos" who were reporting for no-one but who just wanted to be part of it. There were dysfunctional figures who had somehow bluffed their way in as humanitarian aid workers. There were tired local prostitutes and shady black marketeers. There were also some of the most talented and respected journalists of the Western media. Among the most flamboyant was a Swiss radio journalist who abseiled down the central atrium to the breakfast room. He was a dapper character who wore a mod-style suit, winkle-picker shoes, Buddy Holly glasses and a sharp haircut. He also sported a long cheroot. His Alfa Romeo had "Fuck You, I'm Indestructible" plastered on the outside. He was not indestructible, he was later wounded.

Baptism of Fire

My first introduction to the hotel was with Miki Kurilic. We sprinted to it by way of a side street. If you were on foot back then, you had to come in through a kitchen window. I'll never forget the fear of that dash. You did it in two stages. First the run down to the shelter of a shot-up bus. And next, after catching your breath, the chicken run across open ground to the kitchen entrance.

My final journey into Bosnia was in September 1994. This time it was in an armoured Land-Rover, hired from Britain's Sky Television. Bosnia would be a different scene altogether from the one I'd known. The journey down the striking Adriatic coast and up through central Bosnia was peaceful. The Bosnian Muslims and Croats had formed a "federation" earlier in the year. They were no longer fighting one another. It felt like a walk in the park. We drove in behind the first contingent of New Zealanders on their way to join the UN peacekeeping force in what is known as the Vitez pocket. No shooting, no roadblocks. An unnatural calm over the wooded hamlets and shattered villages. A final journey into Sarajevo lay ahead, but even that would be nothing compared with the earlier tours. We would be frightened, yes. There were instances of the odd stray gunshot nearby, but, apart from that, nowhere near the danger I expected. So, even when our Land-Rover broke down on the return journey out of Sarajevo, some 10 kilometres south of Kiwi Company in Santici, it was with barely a second thought that I hitched a ride with a local motorist back to the New Zealand base for assistance. Major Dave Gawn, the Kiwi commander, thought I was crazy.

Was it all worth it? I strongly believe it was. Eye-witness accounts of the injustice and inhumanity still going on in Bosnia are an essential means of sparking our consciences and determination to do something about it. Though, in saying that, I also recognise that those stories have been flowing daily from the Balkan states since the civil war began, and still the barbarism continues. Are we then, the foreign correspondents, little more than voyeurs or vultures feasting on the misery of it all? Certainly, there are Bosnians I have met who once welcomed outside journalists as the world's ears and eyes on their plight, but have now come around to thinking just that.

For me, the role of war correspondent, limited as it was, is the most compelling, urgent and intense experience a journalist can have. In no other arena are you exposed to so full a gamut of the human condition – its passion, intolerance, courage, fear, brutality, humanity and indifference. There is no other assignment I can think of on which you are so forced to examine your own values, your own abilities to operate in danger, your own character.

It's addictive, there's no question of that. There's a club of international media people who spend their lives hopping from war to war. For me, too, the sheer excitement and reality of it all, relative to the trivial concerns of my own life, was a rush like no other.

Would I do it again? The answer would have to be "Yes."

THE JOY AND DESPAIR OF AFRICA

The Rwandan Exodus

Cameron Bennett

It was the sheer scale of the tragedy in the camps straddling the Rwanda-Zaire border that was so personally difficult to cope with. Nothing could have prepared me for what I'd see. This was truly a vision of the Apocalypse – the near-dead and dying huddled in the dust for as far as the eye could see; bodies, in their hundreds, wrapped in the rush mats that had been their shelter, laid out every morning by the roadside, side-by-side like a blown-over picket fence. The death rate was so high that all the existing mass graves were full. This was Goma, a town on the edge of Lake Kivu that few had heard of before the Rwandan crisis. Now Goma was synonymous with the most tragic exodus of modern times. In the space of just five days, 1.2 million people had staggered here to escape retribution after the tribal genocide in Rwanda.

I had flown in with one of our bureau cameramen, Peter Watts, better known as Wattsy. It was no ordinary flight. The aircraft was a Russian charter, an Illushyin 76, hastily painted in the white and red of the International Committee of the Red Cross. We'd brought in only what we could hand-carry; camera, batteries, beta tapes, battery belt and light, tripod, gas burner for cooking, dehydrated food, water purifier, medical kit, a two-man tent and sleeping bags, a few clothes and a pair of boots. We had flown from an RAF base in Kent, on to Cairo and then here, to Goma.

Finding places on a flight at all had been a lucky break. In casting around for seats, I'd checked in with a friend of mine, Nik Toksvig, manning the foreign desk at Sky. Nik and I were mates from when I worked with him at Worldwide Television News in London in the mid-1980s. He secured two places for me on what was one of the first ICRC flights out of Britain. When every major news agency at the time was fighting to get their people on flights, this was some coup.

After hours of delay, we were on our way, hunched in a cargo bay among massive pallets of relief supplies. There was a bench to sit on which folded down from the fuselage wall, but it left us with barely enough room for our legs. The crew had no interest in international safety regulations for passengers. There were no safety belts and the half-dozen journalists on board met with only a "suit yourselves" shrug of the shoulders when we sprawled out on top of the pallets for take-offs and landings.

After an eight-hour delay in Cairo – the Russian pilot took that long to negotiate a re-fuel – we were away again, swooping low over the Nile and across the barren expanse of Africa. The Illushyin's fuselage was sweltering hot; the crew flew stripped down to their underwear. I had been in a Hercules transport before, but this machine felt like it was from another era – no sophisticated on-board electronics, the lining may well have been asbestos and the wiring looked dangerously exposed. Where the plane had come from, I still don't know. Amateurishly painted on the outside was the name "Moscow Airways". No-one I was travelling with had ever heard of it. At least the pilots and navigator knew their business. All had flown for the Soviet air force.

It was nightfall when we finally arrived in Goma, the Illushyin bumping down the runway into what seemed like a dense sea fog. That fog turned out to be a cloud of smoke and dust, not just kicked up by the tens of thousands of feet but also a cloying, black haze spat out by a nearby volcano. We skirted around the customs building and pitched tent in a small media canvas compound that was setting up beside the terminal.

The following morning we were exposed to the full extent of the catastrophe, and all that was separating us from it was a barbed wire fence. Just metres from our tent were six bodies waiting for collection. There were families huddled around fires with literally nothing but the flimsy clothes they wore; children with dead eyes and outstretched hands.

There were people everywhere, milling around aimlessly, squatting by roadsides, on city roundabouts. There was a constant stream of humanity on the move; these were the survivors of the long march from Gitarama or Kigali, the survivors of disease and hunger and attacks by the Rwandan Patriotic Front.

Just down from us was the European Broadcasting Union (EBU) tent, which handled all satellite traffic. I discovered from them that CNN had block-booked the satellite for an enormous sum and would probably be sub-leasing air time at a high price. As it turned out, our own satellite schedule did not conflict with theirs. Telephoning the office is also a problem in locations like this. Portable satellite phones have revolutionised communications and are always in place if a satellite dish is. The difficulty is booking your calls, because there is always an exceptionally long queue. It's expensive too; calls can cost up to $US25 a minute, and the meter starts ticking as soon as the number connects.

The EBU facility was being manned by staff from the Cyprus-based company Newsforce. They were doing it hard. Dust which constantly clogged the equipment also caused the team to suffer bronchial disorders. For weeks on end they worked day and night putting out satellite feeds. Their own living conditions, like ours, were a good deal more basic than a camping holiday in the bush.

My first jobs that morning were to establish where the facilities were; the UN press briefings, the refugee camps, the non-government aid groups like Medicin Sans Frontier (Doctors Without Borders). There were Kiwis here, too, somewhere; Trish Sarr from Oxfam and Heather MacLeod from World Vision. I also needed to hire a car and driver. The going rate was around $150 a day, plus petrol. The Zaireans knew a good thing when they saw it. There was big money to be made out of this suffering.

I found Heather McLeod shortly before she was due to make an assessment of one of the camps. She was like a light in this darkness. I'd met Heather for the first time in Craiova, Romania, in May 1993. She was helping establish care programmes for orphanages in that ugly industrial town. It was a lonely life. To me, Heather was an unsung heroine, because the news interest in the tragic lives of Romania's abandoned and orphaned children had long since passed. There was an extraordinary devotion and commitment to what she was doing. But, being a nurse, she was not the public face of World Vision, and had therefore not received the limelight. My crew and I felt enriched by her company. As an observer and reporter you feel very much the non-contributor, the non-helper in the company of people like that. And here she was again, preparing to do it all over in the most miserable of conditions. Heather's immense task was to join the effort to help relocate an estimated 150,000 lost and abandoned children with their families.

Wattsy and I went with Heather to one of the bleakest of Goma's refugee camps. It felt like God had turned his back on this place. The living and the dead clung to the brown dirt and ugly black volcanic rocks. People were cheek to jowl. I remember stepping out into the throng and standing on a dead body. In any direction there were bodies and the weak groans and listlessness of those about to die. There was dust and smoke and heat. There were blowflies glued to eyes, mouths and noses of the living and the dead. The back of your throat stung, your eyes ran. I grabbed for the motorcyclist's mask I'd bought in London to filter out the smoke and the misery. Its worth was as much psychological as anything else; a brief chance to escape.

On a central plot of land, hundreds more bodies were laid out in their sleeping mats. Western medics were desperately trying to help, but what could they do? There was some food but not enough, and no water. There was no shelter. People were dehydrated, exhausted and starving.

It was a living hell. The evidence was anywhere Wattsy chose to point his camera. There were babies crawling beside their dead mothers. I saw one young boy watching on impassively as his father died. People shuffled like zombies in search of somewhere to rest. We looked for Heather and found her in tears of disbelief. She headed off towards a medical tent for children. Peter was shooting aid workers offloading a truck at the time. I grabbed him and we chased after her. No sooner had we caught up than she stooped in among a pile of rocks. Nestled there in the full blaze of the sun was an infant, abandoned just a few metres from a medical tent. I thought the baby was dead, but Heather knew otherwise. She picked it up and there was a pitifully weak groan. We captured that moment on film; one small moment of compassion. Whether the child lived or died I do not know, but that moment was analogous of the bigger picture. There was just too much misery and not the facilities to cope with it. Whoever had left that baby among those rocks to die need only have carried it a few metres more to the nurses in that medical tent.

I remember going back to the press enclosure and crawling into our tent with my notebook, looking for some respite and the words to do justice to the horrors we had witnessed.

Life for Wattsy and I, although nothing like that of the people on the other side of the barbed wire, was basic too. Just finding a toilet was not easy. The French military had made available one or two of their latrines for the entire press corps, but they became overloaded and were in turn temporarily closed. We could wash our teeth and faces at an open sink, after the military had finished with it. Huge bladders of water had been flown in for that purpose.

You never knew who you might run into at the sink. On one occasion I was standing beside a British TV reporter who was feverishly washing his hands and arms. He had "saved" an abandoned baby by cradling it in his arms and taking it to a shelter. This was a central part of his story, of course; reporter involvement. But, having done that, he was desperately worried he might contract some disease. It seemed to me a disgraceful stunt, when out in the camps nurses and doctors from the aid agencies were putting their lives on the line every minute, and not for the benefit of the cameras. Then again, maybe that reporter's action saved that baby's life.

The media corps was the usual, wildly-varied collection. Agency camera operators who had the look of Euro-hippies, Americans who still managed to look neatly groomed despite the conditions, old hands who'd covered death and disaster from the Congo to Afghanistan. At one UN press briefing I found myself more captivated by a somewhat strident American reporter popping questions than the droning spokesman. This woman looked immaculate when all of those around her looked like wrecks. How was it possible for her hair to be just so? Where had she managed to apply a full face of makeup? How was it that her *Out of Africa* fatigues looked so crisp? I discovered later that she even astounded her own colleagues by pulling out a make-up kit and liberally applying cosmetics to her face in the middle of one of the refugee camps!

Our own problems were more basic. The worst that can happen to a television crew is a camera breakdown. Without a camera there are no pictures and, therefore, no story. It happened to us in the middle of the assignment. The viewfinder had clogged with dust and wouldn't function. Ours wasn't the only camera to break down like that but, unlike the other crews, we had no back-up. Wattsy pulled the viewfinder apart and did his best to clean and reassemble it, but no joy – it was kaput. What to do next? The nearest outlet for camera equipment was Nairobi. It would cost us days if we went there.

Enter Tony Brooks, a former TVNZ sound recordist in Wellington who was then working with Newsforce. Tony is one of a new generation of what are known as "robo-producers". They are expected to be able to shoot, record, edit, repair equipment, set up satellite facilities and produce items. They travel from hotspot to hotspot and are well paid for it. Tony came up with a solution to our problem; a viewfinder that had been discarded by a BBC crew because of a faulty tube. It transmitted a skinny, elongated image, but at least it was an image. Wattsy was able to continue with the assignment.

Editing was also immensely difficult. There were very few edit packs, and they were forever breaking down because of the dust. Clouds of it would constantly blow over the media enclosure, whipped up mostly by the steady stream of relief flights coming in and out. With the enclosure being so close to the runway, there was no escaping the grit or the noise.

So much of getting the job done on the road is about who you know. In my three years in Europe, I'd struck up aquaintances with a fair number of broadcasters and that helped. Many of the contacts were those introduced to me by Robert Penfold, my former colleague from Australia's Channel 9. As he had discovered, you couldn't presume to walk into a situation and hire editing time, or any other technical help for that matter. Most broadcasters solved the problem by bringing in their own. We did when we had to, but because of budgetary constraints, we tended to arrange what facilities we needed on the road. There's no doubt that it saved excess baggage charges, and frequently allowed us to be more mobile, but it could make the task of getting a report to air fraught in the extreme. On many occasions it was literally a case of begging, borrowing or downright theft of editing pairs.

A big help in smoothing the way to a grovelling request to borrow someone's broadcasting equipment was a bottle of whisky. It certainly helped me in Goma. On one occasion where we desperately needed editing time, I slipped a bottle to an editor from Britain's Channel 4. Given the trying conditions we were all living under at the time, that bottle was like liquid gold. The editor recognised that I had made the supreme sacrifice (spirit liquor was not for sharing in Goma) and was forthcoming with his equipment.

Perhaps the most unusual method I employed for securing footage from another broadcaster was in Baghdad, in February 1993. My cameraman and I had travelled overland in a jeep from Amman, Jordan, ostensibly to report on New Zealanders involved in the destruction of Saddam Hussein's chemical weapons arsenal. The Iraqi authorities refused us access to the plant, which meant I had to find vision from somewhere else. Another broadcaster in Baghdad – no names mentioned – had that footage. The deal I struck with the producer was access to the footage in exchange for teaching him the guitar riff to Eric Clapton's *Tears from Heaven*.

Operating in the horrific isolation of the Zairean border, I had no idea what a wave of compassion this tragedy had sparked back home. My first wind of it was a decision by my news editors to air an hour-long special. It was a big commitment with satellite links out of London, Geneva and Goma.

Producing a show like that is an enormous undertaking. I knew all too well what a scramble would have been going on at TVNZ's foreign desk to make the satellite bookings and, once they were made, to establish clear video and audio links. It's a nerve-wracking business, certainly when you are bringing in feeds from remote places. Invariably something goes wrong, which results in a frantic scramble to repair things. It's nerve-wracking, too, when you are the person waiting to go live at the other end of the link. The clock is ticking – sometimes with less than a minute before on-air time – and your technician is still desperately attempting to establish audio links. There have been many times when I have launched into live shots with Richard Long or Judy Bailey and barely been able to hear what their question line was. There is always a delay on the line, which explains the hesitation of reporters abroad in answering questions from the studio.

Goma was no different. I was sprinting back and forth from the live-shot position to the EBU tent to help facilitate the feeds. That might go some way to explaining why a foreign correspondent's composure may not be quite as it should be when conducting live crosses.

The "live" position at the media enclosure in Goma was right beside a perimeter fence. Just out of frame, on the other side of the wire, there would always be six or more bodies laid out. I still have the graphic image in my mind of one man who had crawled his way there and died, his arms and legs still stretched in the mid-stride position that his body had given up on. He lay like that for a full day. At the time, it was the French soldiers and aid workers who were disposing of the bodies. Refugees refused to do it.

One of the aid workers behind that project was an ebullient Irishman by the name of John O'Shea. He established and ran an aid agency called GOAL. As outrageous as he was profane, for years he had cajoled politicians and the public into donating funds to projects anywhere from Mozambique to Somalia. He is the antithesis of the do-gooder but there are few men who do as much good. He managed to score a couple of satellite calls on my account; how could I say no? Aid workers, in my experience, are a curious collection of people. Some are motivated by sheer altruism, others by tax-free dollars, and there are those who are simply looking for an escape from their First World lives. Aid is big business for the non-government agencies. They are often falling over themselves to offer help. In Bosnia there were some 30 agencies operating when I was there. It's exciting, on-the-edge work with very tangible rewards.

On one evening, John O'Shea invited a group of us back to the house his agency was renting. Inside they were looking after a number of abandoned children. In true Irish spirit, O'Shea offered us hospitality. He had a supply of beer from a local brewery. It was an evening of intense debate; O'Shea effing and blinding about this official or that, or this government or another which had failed to respond to one crisis or another. He sent us off with a crate of beer to be passed on to another crew; no inconvenience for us. And it wasn't, until our car broke down in the town of Goma. We were still some four kilometres away from our tent. Wattsy and I set off on foot down the main street on either side of the beer crate. It was a deeply disturbing trek; not because of what we could see, which wasn't much because it was pitch black. What was so disturbing were the sounds; the coughing and the death rattles of people sprawled out on footpaths and on verges.

Our own air force joined the international relief corridor. The government ordered a Hercules to help in the airlift. With that decision made, I was dispatched from Goma to Uganda where the Hercules was due to arrive. If only it was that easy. There were no scheduled flights out of Goma to Nairobi; relief planes were the only flights coming in and out, so you put your name down with the French military authorities for a place on one of them. That could mean waiting hours by the sweltering tarmac only to find out the flight on which your place had been reserved was delayed by 24 hours.

Even in Nairobi, when trying for a connection to Entebbe, it was a bun-fight. Air Uganda's reservation service did not appear to actually extend to reserving a seat. We joined a queue of frustrated travellers. As the flight time drew closer, the queue disintegrated into a shouting match with people offering cash sweeteners to the desk clerk if he could get them aboard.

The New Zealand flight staff and support crews were already in place in Uganda. The position where they'd set up base could not have been more historical. Tents were pitched under the abandoned Boeing that had been at the centre of the famed Israeli raid of 1975. I remember how it was the front-page lead in the *Northern Advocate* when I worked there, and now here I was, where it all happened. The plane had been largely stripped, but it was quite something to be able to clamber through the passenger compartment and cockpit. The old control tower was still there, and still wearing the pockmarks shot into the masonry by Israeli commandos. Other Hercules were assembling there, too, while outside the new terminal was an enormous Antonov – the world's biggest aeroplane – and a US Galaxy, almost as large. But the aircraft were going nowhere. There was a desperate shortage of fuel, and the desperate need for more efficient co-ordination of the airlift.

Coupled with that, there were not enough pallets of

relief supplies for the New Zealand Hercules to ship in. All eyes were on Captain Graham Lintott, the mission commander. The frustration of coming this far and not being able to join the relief effort was immense.

For Wattsy and I, the hotel at Entebbe was luxury after our tent. So was the food. I thoroughly enjoyed the grilled fish, freshly caught on Lake Victoria. I went off it just as rapidly when someone asked why I thought the fish were quite so fleshy. I didn't need the answer. Thousands of bloated corpses had been washed down the Rwandan waterways to the lake, posing a serious risk for local fishing communities.

Delays over a flight schedule were posing a real problem for me. I was under pressure to pull out if the Hercules looked like being delayed indefinitely. Word finally came through that there was a load of soya bean in Johannesburg. That was good enough for Captain Lintott. After clearance from New Zealand we were on our way.

Military Hercules are about as utilitarian as flying gets; apart, that is, from a "Moscow Airways" freighter. There is just the gaping hold and a few webbing stretchers and seats. The toilet is a PVC tube that extends from the wall. Privacy is only ensured by people turning their heads the other way. I was content to spend the journey reading novels; light relief after the rigours of Goma. We arrived in Johannesburg at night and I quickly recorded a piece-to-camera and interviews with the crew before Wattsy and I headed into central Johannesburg to edit together a package and satellite it home. It was a late night for us after the journey. First thing the next morning, the plane was loaded and we were on our way back up Africa.

By late afternoon the Kiwi Herc was making its descent over Lake Kivu and in to Goma. The runway at Goma airport also happened to be a thoroughfare for refugees. They made way for the landing aircraft just in time. Children even played chicken with the incoming and outgoing flights.

Amid the scream of the engines and the swirling dust whipped up by the propellors, the flight crew unloaded the pallets of soya. I dashed off to the side and recorded a piece-to-camera, saying, "This is the tangible evidence of New Zealand's compassion for the refugees of Rwanda." And it was. I felt an immense surge of pride that our country was here helping as well. So did the crew. They all said so in my interviews with them.

No sooner was it unloaded than the Hercules wheeled back onto the runway and prepared for take-off. We were filming as she took off into the dusky haze. I remember feeling a real sense of loneliness. Wattsy and I were back on the ground, on our own again.

Loneliness is a very real aspect of life as TVNZ's Europe Correspondent. On taking up the position, you leave a busy and sociable newsroom for a new life of operating on your own, away from that support system. All other staff at the London bureau were Australian, so I used to be delighted when an assignment meant that I would connect with fellow New Zealanders; but those jobs were few and far between.

It was a shock, even after a few days, to be thrown back into Goma. The press enclosure had doubled in size and the atmosphere felt that much more dusty and smoky.

Cholera had now been added to the horror. People were dying at a rate of up to 3000 a day. It was as if this place was being visited by plague of biblical proportions. Even the nearby volcano, spitting ash and dust as it was, helped reinforce the feeling that the misery here was some sort of divine retribution for the evil that had transpired in Rwanda.

Yet, for all the dehydration, disease and hunger, there were refugees who looked fit. They were, of course, the remnants of the Hutu army. You would see them in groups on the road or in the camps. Their commanders were already plotting to overthrow the victorious RPF. But even more sinister was the propaganda campaign they were waging. They had successfully convinced the starving refugees that to return over the border would mean certain death at the hands of the Tutsis. Despite UN assurances that returning refugees would be protected, few were prepared to risk it; preferring instead to take their chances with disease and famine here than harvest the crops that were already starting to rot across the border.

The Rwandan Exodus

There were probably other reasons for their reluctance. At one of the border crossings we filmed a trickle of people who had quit the camps and decided to take their chances with the RPF. On either side of the road were piles of machetes, axes, grenades and ammunition; the weapons which had been used to slaughter some 500,000 people in the tribal frenzy which took hold in Rwanda. There were more than a few guilty consciences in the refugee camps.

My time here was almost over. My last report was an attempt to follow the New Zealand-delivered aid to its destination. I wasn't able to achieve that, but reported on the sort of places it would be sent. One was an orphanage, which would be one of the most distressing experiences I would have – fly-blown children squatting in the most miserable conditions, their stomachs bloated from lack of food, their parents dead and probably buried in a mass grave. I could barely stand it. I too am a parent, with two young sons.

By now, the story of the refugee camps was moving down-bulletin internationally. Already, news crews at the press compound were discussing the logistics of expeditions into Rwanda itself, not to assess the resettlement of refugees or the post-trauma of Tutsi survivors, but to establish whether the famous Rwanda gorillas had survived the onslaught.

Our journey out was aboard a CARE agency Cessna. We'd been waiting all day for a plane that didn't come. I'd paid extortionate departure fees, in cash, to the airport customs people and was in a sullen mood. Fed up with the wait, I scouted around the tarmac for any plane that looked like it might be leaving. We had to leave that afternoon if we were to make a late connecting flight to London in Nairobi. We just wanted to be out of there. I had seen the CARE plane earlier and arranged seats on it. The pilot said he would alert us when he was departing. He didn't. It was only when I saw his propellors spinning at the far end of the runway that I realised he was leaving without us. Wattsy and I grabbed our equipment and staggered through the shimmering heat to the plane, arriving just in time. There was one last formality before leaving – another cash departure fee to a Zairean airport official.

I've been asked since how I coped with the experience of the refugee crisis. My conclusion is that as a journalist in a situation like this you cannot afford to allow yourself to be paralysed by the horror of it. Just as you can't afford to be paralysed by fear in Bosnia. You just have to get on with it. In that sense, I suppose, foreign correspondents are not dissimilar to aid workers.

At the end of this assignment, TVNZ offered me trauma counselling. It came as a surprise. Counselling had never been offered before, not even after Bosnia. "No," I said. "I'm all right." But I wasn't. Not really. I knew that when I sat alone in a hotel room in Nairobi watching TV and waiting for the flight to take me back to London; CNN was screening more images of the horror I had just witnessed. When I was there, I was all but emotionally shut down. I had to be to get the job done. But here, in this hotel room, it couldn't be shut down any longer. Tears for what I had seen and what I had left behind splashed down my cheeks. I felt utterly bereft, drained and numb.

The following night, I was sitting at a dinner party in London.

The World's Most Famous Prisoner

Liam Jeory

I had always been fascinated by South Africa, not because of any great admiration for the country, but rather because of an inbred dislike. My grandfather, Jimmy Mill, was a halfback for the 1924 All Blacks, the "Invincibles". He died before I was born, and I idolised his memory. That he was not allowed to be selected for the inaugural 1928 All Black tour of South Africa because of the "colour bar" angered me from a very early age. The idea of anyone not wanting to play rugby with my grandfather because he was Maori infuriated my sense of justice. Given that my mother was a founding member of the Halt All Racist Tours movement, and the numerous black and coloured South Africans who visited our home during lecture tours of New Zealand, it should be apparent why I carried a lot of emotional baggage with me when I was sent to South Africa to cover the release of Nelson Mandela.

I remember thinking to myself, "I wonder what a living god is going to look like?" That is not a blasphemous remark. It's just that Nelson Mandela was certainly the most famous prisoner in the world, a man upon whom a movement was based. And no-one had seen his face or heard his voice for 28 years. I was going to the country which barred entry to my grandfather, to cover the release of the man who was to destroy apartheid. Somehow it seemed fitting.

It's a long flight from London to Johannesburg. For the first hour or so it seemed endless. It was my misfortune to be sitting next to a Frenchman who suffered from the worst case of body odour I have ever encountered. There was much humour, at my expense, from Robert, Drew and Richard, for once again this was a joint Television New Zealand/Channel 9 operation. I could see nothing funny about the prospect of sitting next to this man for 12 nauseating hours. After a short while, as his smell permeated the cabin, neither could they.

Eventually, in desperation, I called the flight attendant. All I had to do was talk quietly so she was forced to lean over my smelly neighbour. She quickly cottoned on. A short while later she returned, shook Monsieur Odour and announced that "this was his lucky day. There was room in first class, and he had been chosen for an upgrade." I resolved then and there never to shower for some weeks before a long flight.

The South Africa of 1990 was still very much in the grip of apartheid. I expected, therefore, to find a strictly run, law-abiding sort of place. I was somewhat surprised to be warned upon arrival in Johannesburg that this was an extremely dangerous city. As soon as we checked into our central city hotel we were warned, in no uncertain terms, not to venture out alone at night.

We didn't. But a Swedish journalist who'd arrived that same night did. He took an after-dinner stroll around the block. He arrived back in a dreadful state. His nose was bleeding, an eye was black and starting to puff. His face was cut and his clothing torn. He'd been given a terrible beating. The duty manager rushed to his side to tend to him with words along the lines of "You have to be careful of all the black criminals who pick on people like you." To which the Swede replied, "I was attacked twice. The first time was by two black men who took my wallet. And then as I was making my way back here I got jumped by some white guys. And when they found I had no money, they beat the shit out of me." Another myth exploded. Not all the criminals were black, not all the whites were rich.

The World's Most Famous Prisoner

The imminent release of Nelson Mandela was the worst kept secret of the year. I had gone to South Africa not knowing exactly when he was going to be released, just that it had to be soon. Everyone was treating it as a fait accompli, including the white right and the leader of the Afrikaner Resistance Movement, Eugene Terre Blanche.

His was the most extraordinary press conference I have ever attended. Bear in mind that he called it, and then proceeded to lecture us in Afrikaans. I understood not a word, and neither did the rest of the international media. Afterwards I asked him would he please speak to me in English? I could not believe his reply. In perfect English, he said to me, "I don't speak English." Which was funny, as I'd seen and heard him on television a thousand times speaking it, indeed addressing mass rallies. So again I asked him and explained that I didn't understand Afrikaans. "That, my friend, is your problem. But, just this once, I will make an exception."

And off he went, ranting and raving about how his forefathers had spilt blood to make this land safe for the white folk, for his children and his children's children, and how "blood will flow" the night they release Mandela. And as he went on, all I could think was how Terre Blanche had recently been sprung, having sex on the steps of his beloved Vortrekker Monument with a leading South African gossip columnist who was certainly not his wife.

The whole episode might have been laughable except for the fact that he and his cronies were all dressed in paramilitary khaki fatigues with huge pistols slung around their inevitably large bellies. They looked like throwbacks to the Boers of the Great Trek – an image which, no doubt, they cultivated.

It got completely ludicrous when the conference ended and we wanted to get some pictures of Terre Blanche and his bodyguards walking down the street. They wanted the pictures taken but couldn't bring themselves to be pleasant about it. They marched off, three abreast, down the middle of the Pretoria footpath. No-one was remotely interested in mobbing Terre Blanche, let alone asking for an autograph.

But being ignored doesn't look good. So his bodyguards were walking out of their way to push people around, trying to make it look as though they were hard at work protecting their beloved leader from the eager throngs. It was all I could do to control myself when one of the bodyguards executed a neat little pirouette and began walking backwards, straight into a lamppost.

Terre Blanche was going to have to wait a little longer for his rivers of blood. The American politician Jesse Jackson was in town. There was no way the South African government was going to release Nelson Mandela so long as Jackson was around to grandstand and try and claim some credit. So for a number of days I had to find other things to keep myself occupied. It wasn't hard.

The rebel English cricketers were also visiting Johannesburg, providing quite a focus for black protest. I thought that would be an interesting story, especially as there was talk of a rebel All Black tour. What sort of reception might rebel rugby players expect? Where once rebel tours had passed largely unprotested, it was apparent that those days were over. The black majority would no longer stand by and let them happen.

The cricket authorities and black protesters were engaged in a battle of images. Outside the Wanderers ground, hundreds of black and coloured protesters; inside the ground, hundreds of black cricket lovers. Except, none were watching the game. In fact, many seemed to be asleep or, at least, profoundly uninterested.

Walking outside the ground, at one side I found buses pulling up and disgorging large numbers of bewildered black workers. They were being given tickets and told to go inside the ground and sit on one side, the side opposite the television cameras. They had been hired for the day to help give a good image for South African cricket. The propaganda battle in those days was crude and, as I was to find, sometimes brutal.

Being a member of the international media was a protection in itself in the South Africa of 1990. Most black South Africans felt a debt of gratitude to international journalists for bringing their struggle and suffering to the world's attention. To travel safely around most trouble spots we simply had to tape "TV" and "MEDIA" in large letters on the windows of our vehicle to ensure safe passage. We roamed Soweto at will, going to places that many whites had said would get us killed.

So it was I found myself at an ANC funeral with Winnie Mandela; the funeral of the fiance of Nelson Mandela's daughter. He had died in police custody a week or so earlier and this event was intensely political. I asked the family and Winnie Mandela if we were welcome. We were. In order not to be too intrusive, I stayed in the background while Drew and Richard went in closer to film. I figured I'd just take notes and observe from a distance, but in my dress jeans and short sleeved polo shirt, my dapper little mo and short hair cut, I looked just like a policeman in mufti. A cop! Uh-oh.

I was in for it, and knew beyond doubt when a black journalist sidled up to me and said, "See those guys over there?" He was talking about four shady looking dudes who were slowly making their way around the back of the crowd towards us. He went on, "I saw you arrive with a camera crew, but they didn't. They think you're an undercover cop spying on the ANC and I heard them discussing how they're going to take you out."

I immediately pushed through the crowd to find my crew, grabbed the microphone and pretended to be preparing to do an interview. I never saw those four men again, and for that I'm eternally grateful, as are my wife and children. I was a little more cautious after that, especially when time came to drive out of Soweto that evening. We were lost. In a black township of some three to five million people, of which no street maps exist, we were completely lost – and, after my experience, feeling a little vulnerable. Finally we stopped at a Soweto version of a corner dairy to ask directions. I stayed hidden while Richard, with his long curly hair and Australian surfie look, went in. I was learning.

The next day was time for a riot. There was to be a victory rally at a central Johannesburg church to which all were invited. In reality it was like a well-rehearsed play, the title of which was *Typical South African Police Brutality*. It really was like a performance in which everyone had a part to play and knew it. First, the rally inside the church, with victory speeches in praise of Nelson Mandela. Long before the talking was over, we, the media, had gone outside to find ourselves the best positions from which to film what we all knew was going to happen next.

Right on cue the crowd began to spill out of the church, while from the other side of the square hundreds of riot police appeared. They lined up and began to advance on the black crowd, which began to dance. "Toi toi" they call it. For the life of me I couldn't figure out what the offence was. But it seemed the policeman in charge didn't like them dancing, and ordered them to stop and disperse. I remember his order. "You have three minutes to disperse." Being a Kiwi, I expected a bit of negotiation, a bit of to-ing and fro-ing. I at least expected three minutes. Not a bit.

After what seemed less than a minute, the whistles blew, the police charged, the crowd ran and all hell broke loose. There were batons going up and down, people struggling to get away, and then everything changed to slow motion. We ran after the police as they swept the square. I remember quite clearly standing next to a large policeman with a very red face as he pulled his pistol from its holster and started waving it around.

"Ohh God," I thought. "He's going to shoot somebody." Just then he saw me – in my pressed trousers, polo shirt, short hair cut and neat moustache. "Don't just stand there man. Where's your baton? Get stuck in."

I resolved then and there, the mo had to go. In the meantime, there was much brutality to film. The police were now targeting journalists, giving them a few good thwacks as well. I was standing behind Drew as he filmed a beating when I saw out of the corner of my eye a policeman running towards us. He had Drew lined up for a full speed shoulder charge. Just as he was upon us, Drew fortuitously stepped aside. The policeman ran past, not knowing that Drew had been standing in front of a concrete bollard. It was a hell of a collision. The report in the paper the next day quoted the local police commander as saying the only casualty was one policeman with a broken leg.

I'd been having a jolly old time in South Africa. But I hadn't come for all of this. I'd come to see the release of Nelson Mandela. Finally, on the 11th of February, F.W. de Klerk announced that Mandela was to be released the next day. I was actually standing outside Nelson Mandela's house in Orlando when the news came through. The international media had set up satellite dishes and viewing platforms outside the house from where we were doing our live reports. As soon as the announcement was made on television, Sowetans ran out of their houses and took to the streets, screaming and singing for joy. It was a sight to behold – one minute a long empty street, the next minute a street party with hundreds of thousands of participants.

Archbishop Desmond Tutu lived a few houses down the street and around the corner from the Mandela family home. So his was the first place I went to after the announcement. If ever there was an occasion where words were not sufficient, this was one of them. He came out to meet us, and I asked him to describe his feelings at that moment. He replied, "Freedom is coming," jumped in the air and proceeded to dance.

The next day Nelson Mandela was released, walking out of prison hand-in-hand with Winnie Mandela. It was an incredible moment. What did the most famous man in the world look like? Would he walk and talk like a normal human being? Would he be bitter after 28 years in prison? Would he forgive? What would his message be to South Africans? So many questions made his first speech incredibly important. His very first words were, "I greet you all in the name of peace, freedom for all."

We raced off to Soweto to join the party outside Nelson Mandela's home. He was making his way up from Cape Town as we filmed the dancing in the streets, the euphoria that eclipsed even that of the day before. I interviewed an old black lady by the name of Flora Ngwenya who lived across the road from Nelson Mandela, had done since before he went to prison. She told me that Mandela was "coming home to release everybody in South Africa no matter what colour". Even the riot police.

I have never witnessed such a spontaneous outpouring of joy as I saw in those few days in Soweto as the people waited for Nelson Mandela to return home. Such were the crowds that his motorcade could barely get through the streets. And all the time I was reporting live from outside his house, pinching myself that once again I was at the very centre of international affairs. In this case, a small yellow brick house belonging to the most famous man in the world.

But still there didn't seem a moment or opportunity for Nelson Mandela to actually speak to his people. So far it had all been through television images and press conferences. The people needed to see their leader in the flesh and hear him for themselves. That opportunity came three days after his release before some 100,000 people at the Soweto soccer stadium. I had been to bigger rallies before, in Czechoslovakia. But this was different, this was scary.

We didn't want to gather in the middle of the stadium with the rest of the world's media; we wanted to get amongst the crowd and see it all from a different angle. Smart move! People around us figured that, seeing as we were media, we'd know how to get in, and proceeded to follow us. We had quite a crowd in tow as we approached ground marshals to help us find a way in. And when they opened a stairwell door to let us in, the crowd behind us surged forward and started to push. We were carried down the stairs before them until we came up hard against another door. The people behind it refused to open up to let us through for fear that the rest of the people would rush them. All the time more and more people were pushing from behind. As the pressure got greater the screaming started and people began to panic. I felt in real danger of being crushed. No matter how much we yelled at people to back out, they kept trying to get in until the pressure seemed intolerable. I don't know how it all ended. I just know

Liam in Moscow, outside the Kremlin.

Lounging soldiers and a relaxed
Liam in post-riot Bucharest.

Cameron Bennett shares a joke with Richard Malone in front of a South African army Caspar before the serious business of reporting on a township rally.

Cameron Bennett and Richard Malone in their Gulf War hand-me-down
flak jackets in Sarajevo, July 1992.

A live cross to TVNZ from the
UN headquarters in Sarajevo, July 1992.

Going "live" outside Nelson Mandela's Soweto house after he walked free.

Robert Penfold and Liam Jeory at a Gulf War demonstration in Jordan.

The moment it was announced Nelson Mandela was to be freed.

Corpses as far as the eye could see on the outskirts of Goma,
Zaire, at the peak of the Rwandan refugee crisis.

A piece-to-camera amid the misery of a refugee camp
on the Rwanda-Zaire border.

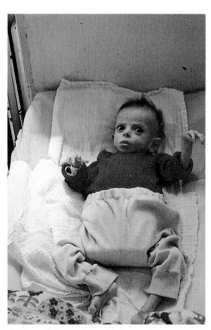

A tiny Romanian Aids
victim.

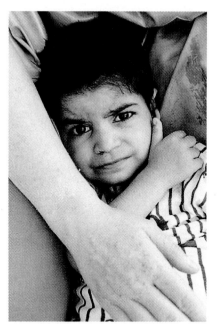

A Gypsy child under the care of
New Zealand nurse Heather
MacLeod in Craiova, Romania.

Smiles, of varying degrees, all round
in a Romanian orphanage.

Standup in front of Buckingham Palace . . . more Royal scuttlebutt.

The coup is over . . . Cameron Bennett and Channel 9's Hugh Riminton watch the withdrawal of the loyalist tank corps from Moscow.

that, after what seemed an age, the pressure went off and we fought our way out of the stairwell and into the fresh air.

So I never got to see Nelson Mandela at his first open-air rally. And after what had just happened, I didn't care. It wasn't a sniper's bullet or a stray mortar round that almost got me. It wasn't anything even remotely exotic at all. Just nearly crushed in a concrete stairwell, in a nondescript soccer stadium on the high veldt.

I ended my South African coverage with a story through the eyes of a young black man called Sam Msibi, a man who'd grown up under apartheid and of whom I asked the question I really wanted to know. Would black people hate or forgive when they got power, as they inevitably would? His answer was one of overwhelming love and forgiveness.

I chose as my ending shots pictures of an ANC casket being lowered into a grave while mourners sang a haunting song that, even today, I remember quite clearly. Over that music and powerful image I said something along the lines of "South Africans of all colours can only hope that, with this casket, they are forever burying their violent past."

POSTSCRIPT:

In 1992 I went back to South Africa. I saw Sam Msibi and asked him did he know the song that so impressed me? "What song?" he asked. I hummed it for him and told him how I had used it to end my South African coverage. Whereupon he laughed and laughed until tears began streaming down his cheeks.

The song was not one of reconciliation and love. Its words went something along the lines of "We're going to cut off their heads and rip out their hearts. We'll fight on forever. We'll never give up." An ANC war song no less.

Free at Last

Cameron Bennett

"Free at last, free at last . . . thank God Almighty, we are free at last." Thabo Mbeke, the man who would become the new first deputy President of South Africa, spoke from the heart at the podium in Johannesburg's Carlton Hotel ballroom on the night of May 4, 1994, when apartheid was declared over.

I was there, in that room, to witness the miracle history had delivered. And it was a miracle; the peaceful transformation of this country against all the odds. It was my Berlin Wall. The atmosphere was elation in a way I had not experienced before. Not the crowing elation that follows a sports victory, but an almost religious ecstasy; it was like a groaning of the heart, a sense that on this night the shame and degradation of generations was over, that an unspoken blessing had been bestowed – the Promised Land. There was spontaneous dancing, there were hugs and there were tears among the movers and shakers of the African National Congress that night.

And then the great man himself, the embodiment of the new South Africa, came onto the stage to claim victory. Nelson Mandela's patrician-like nobility and his humility had me spellbound.

"I stand here before you, filled with deep pride and joy; pride in the ordinary, humble people of this country. You have shown such a calm, patient determination to reclaim this country as your own. And joy that we can loudly proclaim from the rooftops, 'Free at last!'"

It was not so much what he had to say, but that he was here saying it. There was an overriding sense of history in the making. Curiously, Nelson Mandela's speech did not serve to pump up the crowd. He did not dwell on victory. He was generous towards President F.W. de Klerk, the man whose party had been responsible for his imprisonment and the oppression of his people. He appealed to all South Africans to "roll up your sleeves" and "let's get South Africa working".

I had never seen a man of such integrity and righteousness before. Here was this steel-grey-haired septuagenarian, with his erect frame and old-fashioned gentlemanliness, calling for togetherness, not retribution. He, of all people. After all, Nelson Mandela had spent the best years of his life behind bars. On my first visit to South Africa in the 1980s, I remember gazing out from the top of Table Mountain to the squat prison buildings on Robben Island. He would have been there at the time and probably never, in his wildest dreams, thinking that a decade later he would be the first black president of South Africa.

Along with a handful of other TV correspondents who had managed to get into the Carlton ballroom, I waited until his speech was over before recording our piece-to-camera. With Mandela on the stage behind me, jiving to the victory music, and the delirious crowd on the floor joining in, I climbed on top of a chair and reported that moment of victory.

What a privilege it was to be in this company; the ANC leadership and its loyal deputies who'd spent years in exile or detention, suffering brutally for the struggle. These were the people white South Africans had been brought up to hate and fear. These rational and educated blacks, coloureds, Indians and whites had been labelled a bunch of communists, and now they were preparing to take the reins of power.

Afterwards we spilt onto the streets of downtown Johannesburg; the streets where, as a white, you sped through red lights at night and stopped for no-one for fear of being robbed or assaulted. Tonight, there was nothing but joy and goodwill. My cameraman Richard Malone, Channel 9 reporter Hugh Riminton and I were adrift in a sea of black South Africans and treated with nothing but friendliness and respect.

No-one had predicted that Mandela's Rainbow Nation would be born this way. I had expected the worst, as had many others.

April, the month of the majority-rule elections, had begun pessimistically when ANC gunmen had opened fire on supporters of Chief Mangosuthu Buthelezi's Inkatha Freedom Party. Eight of the mainly Zulu Inkatha supporters were killed as they demonstrated outside the ANC's headquarters in Johannesburg. Buthelezi had also introduced the spectre of a potential blood-bath by deciding that Inkatha would boycott the elections.

There was also the ominous threat of disruption by the extreme white supremacists. The ludicrous figure of Eugene Terre Blanche posturing in front of his Afrikaner Resistance Movement (AWB) could not be dismissed lightly. His diehard supporters were not only well-armed, they were apparently well-connected with the police and military. It was into this climate of uncertainty that we arrived, along with hundreds of other international media and United Nations observers.

My first assignment was a landmark meeting in Pretoria in which Buthelezi would announce that he had abandoned his planned boycott. There was a collective sigh of relief for this eleventh-hour reprieve. I was one of dozens of correspondents there. Most were veterans of the years of running battles in the townships, and had the stories to prove it, as we waited in the portals of the Union building, the administrative summit of South Africa, for word of this crucial meeting's outcome.

It was my first look at the key players – Nelson Mandela, F.W. de Klerk and Buthelezi – "in the flesh". Their statement that the election would go ahead with Inkatha's support was flashed around the world within minutes.

The complexities of the South African political

landscape were not new to me. I first visited the republic in early 1984, when international sanctions were at their peak. My wife, Phyl, grew up in Cape Town and it was on that return visit with her that I saw the segregation of the trains, toilets and beaches; was called "baas" by my mother-in-law's black gardener no matter how much I insisted he should call me "Cameron"; saw the immense wealth of the few and the poverty of the many; grew to realise – naive as it may sound – that Afrikaners were not uniformly racist; grew to realise that so-called "English" South Africans were not necessarily the liberal champions that their polite ways implied. And as for my presumption that blacks were uniformly opposed to apartheid, I recall discussing the subject with an ebony-black customs official on the Swazi border. He told me apartheid was a good thing because it ensured racial purity.

If things did not appear as clear cut to me as they should have in South Africa, I later discovered highly politicised, post-Springbok tour Kiwis who laboured under no such confusion. Phyl and I had been working in England at the time of the tour. We arrived back home in March 1986 to find it was still the stuff of raging argument at dinner parties in Wellington, where I had re-joined the Evening Post. People who had not been to South Africa appeared to have remarkable insights into, and solutions for, the place. Phyl, being a South African, often found herself in the position of a social pariah. Dinner guests demanded to know her politics. Their argument was so black and white, so assured. None of them had known what it was like to turn their back on the country of their birth because they opposed its system. Having done that herself, Phyl chose not to grandstand as some sort of political exile.

Limited as my own experience of South Africa was, I had also had some exposure to the passion of black aspirations there. On my second trip to South Africa in the mid 1980s, Phyl and I joined a handful of whites at a rally in Cape Town's coloured suburb of Athlone. It was a moment of high excitement; Ted Kennedy and his family were coming to address the crowd and so was the fiery anti-apartheid activist

Rev Allan Boesak. When the doors to the hall were opened, we were swept off our feet in the rush and propelled forward by the surging crowd. It was frightening; we couldn't have got out even if we wanted to. There were scuffles in the hall, too, involving rival groups.

Ted Kennedy and his family raising their clenched fists appeared disingenuous; the words of a tubby and privileged Bostonian pronouncing on the injustices of South Africa were unmemorable. Allan Boesak, on the other hand, was electrifying. I'd heard the rhetoric before on television, had seen the massed protests. But being in amongst it was a new experience; the sharp smell of mealie-scented sweat, the laughter, the anger. My first real sense of the inevitability of their struggle, that one day they would claim power, came during the massed-harmony of the African anthem, Nkosi Sikelele. It felt like the voice of Africa, an unstoppable force, and set the hairs on the back of my neck on end. At the same time, there was little indication that P.W. Botha's government was on the verge of being overthrown.

I was back in South Africa again in March 1992; this time for work. The occasion was the historic, whites-only referendum over power-sharing with blacks. P.W. Botha was gone, the referendum brought about by F.W. de Klerk. He had little choice. The watering down of the worst aspects of the apartheid laws and the efforts to incorporate blacks into government as junior partners were still not acceptable to the outside world. The sanctions were biting hard.

There was talk of nothing else but the referendum among the whites I met at the time. There were the hardliners, of course, who warned of a communist plot and the inevitable demise of their country – look at what had happened to just about every other country in Africa when the blacks took over? But, in my experience, there was a broader belief that the system needed changing. There was a longing to be brought back into the international fold. There was also the question of a clear conscience. A great number of white South Africans are devout Christians. They had run out of any way to justify apartheid in the context of their faith. For all of that, there was also a tremendous sense of foreboding and a fear of retribution.

Sanctions worked, but they cost. International companies had pulled out under pressure and the level of unemployment was painful. It hurt at all levels. I reported on the emergence of a new breed in South Africa – the poor white. We had pictures of them working side-by-side with black labourers and living off hand-outs. Many of these were people who'd enjoyed sheltered employment on the likes of the state railways. But all that had changed; the subsidised way of life was gone, there was no social welfare, they were on their own. You could feel the effect of sanctions, too, in the look of South Africa. It appeared to be caught in a time vacuum, the Western world long since having passed it by.

There was a tremendous euphoria amongst whites after the "yes" vote to the referendum. Up till now there had not been a clear indication of just how acceptable change would be to the white electorate. In a country which, because of gerrymandering, had for decades been so dominated by the National government, whose press had been shackled by censorship, there was no way of truly gauging white opinion until that historic moment.

It was on that 1992 trip that I made my first visit to the seething cauldron of Soweto. It was another culture, another nation to the one I'd seen in the suburbs of Johannesburg or Cape Town. Endless rows of squat, brick houses and shanties. Four million people lived here in the squalor and dust. This was a culture of jive and chance, of the desperate and the dispossessed; it had its own rhythm. Aphrodisiacs were on sale outside the rough, canvas shebeens – the illegal drinking haunts; all it took was kwela music on a workman's transistor radio for wide-hipped mamas, with their woolly hats and jackets reversed so the labels were on the outside, to shuffle and groove as they waited at the bus stop; deeply committed Pentecostalists crammed into the Toyota mini-van taxis beside gangsters. It was a place where few whites ventured. The dangers were legend; cars being stoned, and the most gruesome revenge of all – the necklace. This was when victims were executed by way of a burning tyre draped around their necks.

My colleague Robert Penfold and I wanted to produce feature stories on the Soweto Flying Squad, the police force charged with the responsibility of trying to keep a lid on all of this. We organised, through a fixer who had contacts in the police, to join the squad for a night patrol.

It was a memorable assignment. We turned up at the highly secure police base in Soweto in time for the konstables' early evening prayers. They were asking for divine protection from the dangers of the night ahead. They needed it. There would have been few more dangerous policing jobs in the world at the time.

Then it was time to move. The squad of four we travelled with were bristling with guns – pump shotguns, semi-automatics and pistols. There was one black officer on board. He was a sergeant and technically the senior officer, but the young, gung-ho Afrikaner konstables paid him only lip service. We were travelling in a Caspar, a fully-armoured truck, designed and built in South Africa, which became internationally synonymous with the suppression of the townships.

It made for dramatic television. The radio was sputtering out information incessantly. Go to this place or that; domestic violence, a robbery, a shooting . . .

But these policemen were foreigners in a foreign land. They were highly vulnerable and, by extension, so were we. The system used when dealing with a situation was that two officers would speak with the complainants while the other two took up point duty with their guns, front and back of the Caspar. In one situation, an angry crowd grew by the minute as the officers attempted to get to the bottom of a car theft. We were parked by empty land that faced directly on to the notorious Zulu hostels, the tenement-like buildings which housed migrant workers and the site of many a shooting. I was nervously aware of that as I held up the battery-powered "sun gun" to direct light for cameraman Richard Malone. Not only did I feel lit up like a Christmas tree, but it would have taken only a couple of people in the crowd with guns to have shot us all. The policemen were aware of that as well, because, for all their weaponry, they could not have taken on a crowd like this.

Richard was just as edgy while following the officers through a room-to-room search of a house. At any time, someone could have emerged shooting. A semi-automatic would have cut down at least one of the officers and probably taken Richard with it.

The final call of the night was to a shooting. There was high excitement in the Caspar. We had no idea whether the gunmen were still holed up at the location. The excited chatter on the radio spoke only of casualties and that semi-automatics were being fired. A group of Caspars swooped on the area followed by house-to-house searches. The gunmen had got away, though. They almost always did. Lying in the back of a pick-up truck were two of their victims, both with gunshot wounds to the stomach.

Just over a year later, I was back in Johannesburg to cover the lead-up and result of the elections. There had been the eleventh-hour breakthrough in the deadlock over Inkatha, but a great deal more suspense was in store before polling. Throughout, there was the threat of trouble by white extremists. It became a shocking reality on a quiet Sunday in central Johannesburg.

At the time of that enormous bomb blast, Hugh Riminton, Richard Malone and myself were on our way to the Orange Free State to report on a town which had plans to fence itself off from the imminent new South Africa. The first we heard of it was a message bleeped to us on a pager.

Nine people dead, at least 100 injured. It had been a car bomb. Gaping holes were left where shops had been; glass and steel had knifed their way through the dust and chaos in a murderous assault on the housewives, children and men who'd come for a leisurely day out.

A Channel 9 crew was close to the scene when it happened. They recorded some of the most graphic images; wailing police cars, a woman cradling a bloodied child, firemen. We got back as fast as we could, though by that time the bodies had been removed. But the evidence was still there; a single woman's shoe, the tattered remnants of a roadside fruit stall – its owner had literally been blown to bits – and the blood stains.

We negotiated our way through the police cordon and I recorded a standup. About the same time, a dazed and bloody survivor returned to look at the carnage. He became a central interview for my report.

The tension in Johannesburg was palpable. In the white suburbs people were buying enormous quantities of groceries and canned goods in preparation for possible civil war. We visited gun shops, too, which were rapidly selling out of handguns, shotguns, ammunition and even flak jackets. Adding to the paranoia were the reports starting to flow in about the appalling tribal massacres in Rwanda. People were bracing themselves for the worst.

By contrast, in the townships, I was amazed by the enormous sense of goodwill among blacks. There was a recognition that changes to their lot would not happen tomorrow, but at least they would happen; housing, jobs, education, that's what Mandela had promised. Those I spoke to talked not of revenge but, like their revered leader, of a shared revival.

Even so, Nelson Mandela himself was faced with awesome difficulties in keeping it all together. I attended an ANC rally in Soweto where he was the key speaker. Thousands had turned out at the football stadium, singing and dancing the toi toi. Well away, there was a strong military presence but no interference. Again, rather than crowing of victory, Mandela admonished his supporters about the need for tolerance for other racial minorities, such as the Indians. His speech turned to cold fury when AK-47 shots of celebration started ringing out from the stands. The gunshots were unnerving for me. All it would have taken was for a disaffected follower to assassinate Mandela or some of his lieutenants and the rally would have disintegrated into a riot.

In the 48 hours after the blast in central Johannesburg there would be a dozen bombings. No-one was admitting responsibility, but already the neo-Nazi AWB was the prime suspect. I reported on another two of them; one was a car bombing that rocked Johannesburg airport on the second day of polling. The blast injured 16 people and tore gaping holes through the concrete and glass exterior and through a ceiling. It was further calculated to unsettle whites, particularly. Witnesses reported a white man fleeing the scene before the explosion.

The second bombing was in the drab, working class suburb of Germiston. This time, a black taxi rank was the target. The damage was horrendous; Toyota vans were crushed and flung on top of each other. The taxi rank looked more like a wrecker's yard. We searched for and found witnesses. Their shaken accounts would end up in the international news pool and feature in bulletins around the world. No-one knew how many people had been killed. I saw a hand lying under a car well away from the blast.

A wave of police arrests followed the spate of bombings, and after that there were no more. Officially, the blasts accounted for 21 lives and scores of injured; a shocking death toll anywhere else, but not in South Africa where life had long since lost its value as a precious commodity.

I was there, too, for the last gasp of the AWB before the new South Africa was ushered in. Supporters had assembled a convoy of cars and pick-up trucks in the northern Transvaal mining town of Rustenburg. The police and military were on full alert, clearly determined to stop any trouble before it started. So much so that our car was tailed by plainclothes officers. We'd arrived early and were reconnoitring the town. The police pulled us over and ordered us out of the car. They were serious. We were frisked by officers whose guns were drawn, and only then freed to join up with the media waiting beside a police cordon blocking the AWB convoy.

The AWB supporters had the look of out-of-control gun freaks; beefy, swaggering hooligans in khaki fatigues rallying beneath the colours of Hitler's Germany. They were loving all the attention. Film crews were shooting them from every direction. The leaders posed and strutted in a quasi-military fashion.

There was another sideshow taking place, too. A fellow reporter from TVNZ, Mark Sainsbury, was also on the spot and was looking to build this event into a feature for Holmes. He managed to insinuate himself and his cameraman into one of the convoy's lead pick-ups. It all turned into high farce when Sainsbury, all flowing handlebar moustache and Akubra hat, was himself mistaken for an AWB man by European TV crews, who attempted to interview him. He was perplexed by the association with the Afrikaner Resistance Movement stormtroopers, especially considering he'd worn a lurid, candy-striped shirt that day to avoid any such confusion.

The convoy was finally given clearance; they set off for a rally outside the home of the founder of the Afrikaner nationalist movement, Paul Kruger. Tailed by media cars, the convoy turned into a high-speed game of chicken. Media cars were ducking and weaving in and out of the convoy, the AWB supporters speeding and slowing; tyres were hurling up rocks from the roadside shoulder and a couple of cars even crashed.

It was a sweltering afternoon. The media contingent lugged its equipment up into the grounds of Kruger's home, waiting for the arrival of Eugene Terre Blanche. Squeezed into his fatigues, he announced: "We are Boer people. We are fighters . . . I think there will be more explosions and more actions if the government of my people who demand some land." It was dismal. I thought Terre Blanche appeared more as a caricature than a serious figure. Then again, no-one had taken Hitler seriously in the early days.

A black American reporter covering the events was later roughed up and ejected by some of Terre Blanche's khaki-clad thugs.

But away from the hatred and the bombing, something altogether more noble was unfolding. South Africans were flocking to the polls.

We filmed the queues outside the polling booths in Johannesburg and in the heat and dust of Soweto. There, people of all ages had been waiting their turn since before dawn; old men and women in their Sunday best who still could not believe it was happening. There were veterans of the '76 riots; there were men and women who, for all their working lives, had been known as "houseboy" and "the girl"; there were the widows and orphans of the violence; there were sky-larking youths and blushing teenagers tottering in their high-heels and sheltering under their parasols; there was a great dignity and sense of promise that I will never forget. These were the people who for generations had bitterly cried, the Beloved Country. Now the tears were of joy and liberation and the tears flowed freely as ballot papers were cast.

When it was over, the feeling among whites I spoke to was one of immense relief; relief that they could get on with lives that for so long had been on hold. In the years leading up to the referendum and finally the election itself, it cannot be overstated how eroded their society was by despondency over the future; a despondency that caused the steady emigration of friends and family to new lives in places like New Zealand.

My last recollection of that time is of white South Africans. The election all but officially confirmed, we'd finished work for the night and were eating in a popular steak house in suburban white Johannesburg. The place was jumping, the beer was flowing like water, popular hits were blaring out on the sound system and everyone was swaying and hugging and singing along. And then, a more poignant moment you couldn't imagine; Mary Hopkins' 'sixties-era number one and everyone singing like there's no tomorrow:

"Those were the days, my friends,
We thought they'd never end . . ."

The Friendly Invasion

Cameron Bennett

*"Pack your sleeping bag, we're going." Rob Penfold, my
bureau colleague with Australia's Channel 9, has the OK from
Sydney. It's what TVNZ has been waiting for – without the
Aussies to share the costs Auckland is not prepared to go it
alone.*

As American troops are steaming to the Horn of
Africa, across Europe and North America news bureaux
mobilise for a media circus the like of which hasn't been
scrambled since the Gulf War. Already there is talk of the US
networks chartering whole passenger jets and buying up all
the available accommodation. Cameraman Peter Watts,
Robert and I are joining the pack.

Like so many of the really demanding assignments I
was dispatched on, the decision to go was a last-minute affair.

Somalia? Where to start? It's not on the international
tour map. There are no direct flights in. A civil war is raging
there in the wake of one of the most chronic famines the world
has seen. Just getting there will be enough of a challenge, the
journalism will have to look after itself.

It's a strange mix of adrenalin and the jitters that takes
over about now. There is too much to do in too little time for
us to dwell on the dangers. Still, for the three of us, there's no

escaping the fact that we could end up as casualties; Western journalists are already being held up and robbed at gunpoint in Mogadishu. Some will later be killed.

In planning a trip like this, you are on your own. Neither Auckland nor Sydney have the experience to help. In that regard, Rob Penfold was a gift. Seven years a foreign correspondent, he knew the ropes and readily shared his experience. I'd done my share of travelling in the Third World before taking up the London post, but this was something quite different. The lessons I learnt from Rob would prove invaluable on future assignments.

First, thousands of US dollars to be withdrawn from the bureau account. Cash, always cash – you never know if you might have to buy your way out of trouble. Flights to Kenya to be booked, visas, calls to international television news agency WTN about uplink and satellite facilities. I know Auckland will want live shots as well and I know I can trust Chris Mannering, the bureau's satellite manager, to facilitate them. Overweight and cantankerous, even by his own admission, he is a wizard. It's no mean achievement to organise satellite "windows" when the world's networks are clamouring for limited air time. He never failed us.

We know there's no chance of buying food in Somalia. We'll have to carry our own. Dehydrated meals are the lightest option – chicken kormas, beef stroganoff, custard. Fresh water will have to wait until Nairobi, the staging point for all charter flights into the anarchic Somali capital.

No time for booster shots, and we'd be on our way and probably out before they would take effect. Malaria tablets, shortwave radio, Swiss army knife, chewing gum, whisky. And Marlboro cigarettes, the international currency. Offering them around to customs officials, border guards or local militiamen can be the difference between getting past or not.

Everyone has their own routines for packing and I have mine. My kit – money, radio, knife, Maglite torch, toiletries and clothes – is laid out on the bed. The standard routine is to ask aloud: "Passport? Have I got my passport? Tickets?" Without them you are sunk, and all of us on at least

one occasion have had the panicky realisation on the way to
the airport that we've left our documents behind.

Some correspondents and cameramen have their
lucky totems . . . it can be a brightly coloured pair of socks.
Mine is a Wimbledon bag – a media giveaway from the All
England Lawn Tennis & Croquet Club. That bag travelled with
me on assignment from Cape Town to Moscow to Bosnia and
dozens of locations in between.

At Heathrow Airport there's a squabble with Air
Kenya officials over excess baggage. Relative to crews from
other networks we always travel light, and this time is no
exception. Even so, the extra kilograms will cost.

There's a heightened sense of excitement and
uncertainty at the outset of an assignment like this.
Excitement that you are about to join an elite band of
correspondents covering the world's number one foreign
story – uncertainty that you might fail to deliver for some
reason, that your own material may not measure up against
that of the foreign networks. There's another brand of
uncertainty too, a nagging uncertainty that largely goes
unspoken but is with you all the same. What if you're wounded
. . . or worse? No-one goes into a war-zone without giving
thought to that. The pay-off if all goes well – if your reports are
well received, if you've come through unscathed – is a wild
sense of euphoria. That exhilaration is unparalleled.

The Nairobi airport baggage carousel is laden with
television equipment from the world's networks. Waiting for
theirs to glide by are the "shooters", the frontline cameramen
in their scruffy fatigues, denims, Timberland boots, ponytails,
red neck-scarves, "Desert Storm" caps and that bored, world-
weary look affected by just about everybody who frequents
the international hot-spots. One wears like a badge a healed-
over gunshot wound to his arm. I listen in as others re-
establish their credentials in flat monotones. Most recent
assignments: Bosnia, South Africa, Afghanistan . . . and now
this "shit-hole".

We see Mo Amin, the famous Reuters cameraman,
who lost an arm while covering the war in Ethiopia. He's

organising a charter flight to Mogadishu but there's no room for us. If we're to get in at all we'll have to find a plane of our own, and the queue for them is growing.

A fleet of aircraft – twin-engine, single engine, commercial freighters – are parked at Nairobi's second airport, Wilson. The Kenyan heat shimmers off the tarmac, trolley-loads of equipment bank up, bribes change hands, tempers are frayed. The quantity of customs declarations, departure forms and other paperwork is infuriating. It seems as if every small-time flier from central and southern Africa is here for a piece of the action. These are aircraft that operate from Angola to Uganda carrying people and freight, money-up-front, no questions asked.

"It's yours – for $US5000," we're told by a pilot with a heavy Zimbabwean accent. He's got the look of a long-distance truckie; too much nicotine, too many barbiturates to counter those long flying hours. His Cessna looks like it's seen more air miles than it should have. But his is a captive market. With too many news teams for the planes available, charter prices have doubled in less than a fortnight. You take what you can get.

The great spread of continental Africa, as far as the eye can see, drifts past below; squat, flat-topped trees on khaki plains. The Cessna bucks the thermals and updrafts from the escarpments. From the air, the border between Kenya and Somalia is indistinguishable; on the ground they are worlds apart.

Already there is tension in the cabin and we've barely made Somali airspace. Our manic pilot has run out of cigarettes and is rummaging around in his flight bag. "Here, you take the controls," he yells to our alarmed cameraman, who is sitting in the co-pilot's seat. He's not joking. We all desperately rummage for cigarettes. A pack is found and our flaky sky jockey resumes control.

We're sweating, and we haven't even arrived yet. I suppose it shouldn't have come as a surprise. Somalia is no normal destination and this is no normal flight.

"I can't land – they're shooting up the airport!" Our

The Friendly Invasion

edgy pilot makes a low pass over Mogadishu International but is warned off by air traffic controllers. It's late afternoon and the choice is an airstrip some 40 kilometres out of town or to turn back for Kenya. We opt for the airstrip.

The Cessna plunges out of the sky onto a freshly scraped runway. From the windows we can see a collection of trucks and militiamen. We've made it; now we've got to make it past them.

What to do next? How do you transport yourself into town? How safe are the roads? What language will they speak? Being a foreign correspondent is all about handling dilemmas like this. There are no rules and little in the way of advice. More often than not you are literally "dropped in it". Your newsroom has no understanding of that, and is not particularly interested. It's your problem, work it out. There's a newsroom shortform for not delivering a story. It's called an FTD, a "failed to deliver". It's a harsh reality in this business that you either deliver or you FTD. If it's the latter, no amount of excuses to news editors half a world away can prevent that damning judgement.

Through the noise and dust whipped up by the Cessna engines we can barely hear what the militiaman with the clipboard and the Kalashnikov is saying. It soon becomes clear: "You must now give me $US100." Why? "It is the landing fee!"

Welcome to Africa.

Skinny gunmen in hand-me-down fatigues and running shoes have formed a menacing semi-circle around us. We don't argue with the price, of course. But, just for the hell of it, we ask for a receipt. Incredibly we get one.

So now what? Our plane is already banking steeply into the early-evening sky. We are in Somalia and there's no turning back. Just us, our bags, the gunmen and a few dilapidated trucks. Those trucks, we discover, are bound for Mogadishu and we are determined to be on one of them. We have satellite feeds to New Zealand and Australia in about fifteen hours' time. Auckland is collating the latest updates from affiliated broadcasters already filing from Somalia. My biggest task is to make sure I can be there in time to write voice-overs and establish my presence in Somalia with a piece-to-camera.

The truck's lurching wooden flatbed and the fading light provide the platform for the standup. It's a scene-setter. I report that already the warring militias are moving weapons and equipment from the Somali capital to the hinterland in anticipation of the American arrival. It's information gleaned from BBC World Service reports monitored on my shortwave radio.

The soft light of the early evening lends a beauty to this barren landscape that belies its tortured reality. There is no rule of government here, only that of raging gunmen whose fratricide has inflicted starvation on millions of their countrymen and reduced the country to anarchy. It's on this inhospitable turf that our truck breaks down.

The repair will take an hour. The pitch-black African night is alive with cicadas, the whine of mosquitoes and the sound of African voices. It's like a huge and foreign void. There are no lights but for the stars. This is no place for a city boy. My concern is of being set upon by a roving patrol of militiamen, but the worst danger we will face that night is from mosquito bites.

Ahead of us lies Mogadishu and the story that will dominate news worldwide. The old truck lurches once more into the African blackness.

Dirt and discomfort go with the territory on this sort of assignment and we will be short of neither. We establish base in the shell of a house-cum-hotel that has been rented to the European Broadcasting Union (EBU), which facilitates all satellite feeds out of the city. Home is a stone floor and a thin squab. For that we pay $US100 a night, per person. It is one of the paradoxes of Somalia: while poverty and squalor are everywhere, I find myself paying the same price for a hotel bed as I would in London. The building's owner is a corpulent raconteur, one of a number of dodgy businessmen and racketeers who'll pocket a small fortune in the days ahead.

A miserable, makeshift refugee camp is set up right

beside the building and you can be sure our host shared none of his enormous gains with those people. Driven by a sense of guilt, I tossed a number of items over the fence to them – chewing gum, dried biscuits and a TVNZ tee shirt. It was a mistake. A small riot followed as these skeletal villagers traded punches and scratches in the scramble to grab what they could.

I had hoped my friend David Shearer and his wife Anushka, from Auckland, would still be there – if nothing else, for a good meal and a shower. They had been in charge of the Save the Children Operation for the past year but their contracts were over shortly before Operation Restore Hope began. Nevertheless, we paid the SCF compound a visit. Despite my best efforts at name-dropping in the appropriate ears, we never did manage an invitation for dinner or a shower. So it was back to the dehydrated food and the squab on the floor.

The Americans are not due to storm the beaches of Mogadishu for another two days. Now the scramble is on for foreign journalists to provide situation reports and "colour" stories on a city which, in the most bitter months of the civil war, was largely ignored.

Mogadishu is a dusty, sand-clogged collection of streets. It's described in my atlas as a capital city, but don't be fooled. It's like no capital anywhere else in the world. Even in the most beleaguered and broken down capital cities like Sarajevo things work. You can find hotels that function. In between blackouts, lights flicker into life. There are even street signs. But not here. In the Mogadishu I happen upon, nothing works. The water in our building, when it's running, is bracken. One evening, I cut my hand on a tap and was left desperately worried about contracting a disease. Rob Penfold would return to London harbouring a tropical bug that would leave not only him hospitalised, but also his family.

In those days before the Americans arrive, anarchy reigns absolutely supreme. The mean streets could be scenes out of *Mad Max*. People lurk in the shadows of bullet-peppered buildings or on street corners while militiamen – young boys mostly – career across town in cut-down Toyota Landcruisers fitted with heavy machineguns. These mobile killing machines are known as "technicals". Some of them have car stereos that blast out the disco hits which are doing the rounds in the US and Europe – "Let's talk about sex, baby, let's talk about you and me . . ." It seems unbelievable that just a few hours' flight away, kids of the same age are jiving to the same music. Here they kill to it. The stench of rotting corpses from the nearby cemetery hangs heavy in the air near the EBU building. The graves are too shallow, too hastily dug. Already wind and rain has partially exposed the corpses. The gunmen and anyone else who can afford it chew on a weed called "chat". It dulls the senses just enough to keep reality at bay. The gunmen are veterans of daily battles on the frontline that divides Mogadishu. They are the shocktroops of Somalia's apparently compassionless warlords.

Security is our fear. The only way to travel is by pick-up truck with armed guards. Ours are hopelessly ill-equipped for trouble. One guard has a rusty old machinegun with a magazine on the top which looks more like a soup plate. Whether there are any bullets inside we never find out. Our second man has an AK-47 but neither of them look committed to defending us in a firefight. Sitting on the back of the truck, we feel hopelessly exposed. There are any number of guns in town and we are sitting ducks. The TVNZ/Channel 9 operation is put in stark relief when the diminutive figure of American newscasting giant Ted Koppel glides by in a convoy of armed jeeps – he's the sole passenger.

This may be the hellhole of the world, but the American TV people, from what I can make out, want for nothing; vast supplies of equipment and food have been shipped in. Incredibly, one morning a frantic network producer comes to our humble abode in search of a hair dryer. A hair dryer? I was using dry shampoo to disguise my own lank mane. We had only a trickle of running water. We couldn't believe it. Apparently, a network presenter's hair dryer had broken down – they had a crisis on their hands.

The American media posse was something to behold.

The Friendly Invasion

Among them were the truly great names of international reporting, and then there were the local, affiliate-station reporters. These were reporters used to operating in metropolitan Los Angeles and downtown San Diego. They had crisp, new fatigues still creased in squares. They had flak jackets, fishing jackets, khaki cotton jackets. They had boots and buckles – they had the works. These were reporters with sign-offs like "Danny Lopez . . . Channel Seven Action News . . ." These were reporters who never operated beyond stateside and here they were – they may as well have been on the moon.

We ran across a couple spiralling out. "What's this goddamn PAL," they were shouting. PAL is the television format used by most of the world, but the Americans use a system called NTSC. They had no idea about that. They were going to "kick their producer's ass" back in LA. If Rob Penfold hadn't been able to arrange for their product to be fed through our satellite links, they would have FTD'd and their "asses would have been kicked". There is a reporter and story producer out there who owe us.

In one determined show of "looking the part", the affiliate reporters were mingling with the network heavyweights outside the home of clan warlord Mohammed Farah Aidid. A competition seemed to be on over who could outdo the other with sheer, mellifluous depth of voice, sheer basso profundo. The man to scoop the pool was the top NBC newscaster Tom Brokaw. To make matters worse, he was not dressed in fatigues but in a polo shirt. Later that day, I noticed that it was a case of "break out the polo shirts" for the west coast wonder boys.

On December 9, 1992, Operation Restore Hope began. When the first US Marines landed on the beaches of Mogadishu that day, it must surely have been the most televised, most comprehensively reported military operation in history.

The Seal special forces' arrival on the pristine foreshore before dawn is now media legend. Crawling ashore in battle formation, greeted by cameras and lights blazing, their night-vision scopes became overloaded by the halogen bulbs. Across the sand dunes is the airport – it too was ablaze in light. Every major American network was broadcasting live, the invasion coinciding with the primetime evening bulletins on the US east coast.

I remember talking with a couple of British reporters who were determined the operation was typically American, and therefore a shambles. They made great play out of the image of a serviceman tripping head-first into the sand. For all the world it looked like a movie set: tense marines snaking their way over the dunes, doing their best not to acknowledge the battery of camera crews and photographers pointing lenses just inches from their faces. We were there on the beaches as well. I used the backdrop of humvee jeeps disgorging from one of the enormous military hovercraft for my dawn piece-to-camera. If the Brits thought it was a shambles, I thought it was an awesome operation. A whole military infrastructure was being transported into Mogadishu, from computers to field kitchens to hospitals to prefabricated buildings. All day the hovercraft travelled back and forth to the waiting fleet, ferrying in troops and equipment. It went with clockwork precision. Cobra attack helicopters patrolled in pairs. I remember watching them loom in front of us while we stood on a roof top. They looked like the ultimate killing machine – rockets mounted either side and a heavy-calibre cannon on the front. Pity the renegade "technical" that tried to take one on. It was a display of might that would not be lost on the local people either.

As the US troops fanned out across town and the live news shots back to the States wound down, Mogadishu became a carnival. The "technicals" were nowhere to be seen. The AK-47s were neatly buried. Everyone was a cheering civilian.

We no longer needed our own tin-pot armed escorts either. We joined the throngs of people who dogged every move the troops made. Our biggest threat now were the pickpockets. The US camera crews also dogged the soldiers' footsteps which meant there would be no displays of unrestrained behaviour. There was an immense sense of relief in the air. A sense that now the Americans had arrived the country would be restored to law and order, that the killing and misery would stop. It was a sense of goodwill that would be fleeting.

But if the Americans were practising restraint in front of the cameras, the French Legionnaires, who were also part of the operation, had no such inhibitions. I followed them as they made house-to-house searches. I'd heard there was a Kiwi among them – what a story that would have made. I never found him, but I saw first-hand the legionnaires at work. They had no qualms about swatting people with their rifle butts or putting in the boot. I have a lasting memory of one hapless Somali being led away with the muzzle of a legionnaire's rifle firmly wedged up his nostril.

The legionnaires would soon be drawn into a shootout with the locals. Just a short distance from our building, they opened fire on a truck which had failed to stop at a roadblock. I understand two people were killed.

With the Western takeover of Mogadishu, we had much greater access to sectors of the town previously out of bounds. One of the most grotesque sights was not the misery of refugees and townsfolk but the scene at the city's main port. Inside the warehouses were tens of thousands of kilograms of grain. The feuding warlords had stockpiled it there as their own people starved.

Looking at the Americans arrive on that December morning, I firmly believed there was no other choice. Someone had to get food past the armed gangs and out to the desperate hinterland. Graphic TV pictures of a famine that was claiming up to 1000 lives a day fuelled the clamour for something to be done. Whether George Bush responded because he, too, was outraged, or whether he was looking to end his presidency in a blaze of glory, is still debatable. But for starving Somalis, it didn't matter what the motivation was, they were being fed. And, for a while, things went well. The US-led international force managed to open up supply routes and get food shipments moving. They even, for a time, managed to disarm the militiamen. But 10 months later, Operation Restore Hope had gone horribly sour. Soldiers were dying and Americans back home were questioning how it was that a humanitarian intervention to feed the starving had ended in US troops being treated as the enemy.

I did not stay to witness any of that. My brief was only to cover the "friendly invasion" itself. After seven days on one of the most arduous assignments going, we were exhausted. It wasn't just about the trying conditions, but also the hours we were keeping. The time difference between New Zealand and East Africa usually meant editing late into the night, snatching a few hours sleep, and then waking early morning for satellite playouts and live shots.

I have clear memories of our last night in Mogadishu, squatting in the balmy night on the the rooftop of the EBU building. ITN's Jeremy Thompson, a veteran Africa-hand, was presiding over an enormous bottle of whisky. "Time to go home, boys," announced Jeremy. He'd just got word from his foreign editor that Somalia – the story that had led bulletins worldwide – had been "bumped" in London. Another instalment in the Charles and Diana saga had seen to that.

Interest was waning back home, too. News is a fickle business. The Somali crisis had not gone away, but it was time to move on to the next assignment.

IT'S A FUNNY OLD PLACE

UK Tales

Liam Jeory

*My very first day in England started off with one of life's
incredible coincidences.*

My wife, Carol, and I landed in the early morning of
November 14, 1988. An apartment had been arranged for us in
Paddington. Neither of us knew much about Paddington, and
were totally lost by the time the taxi dropped us and all our
luggage off outside the apartment door. After a sleep we were
eager to explore and, just as importantly, to telephone some
dear friends who had recently moved to London from the
United States.

So we went for a walk to the High Street to find a
telephone and ring Deborah and Dave. They answered the
phone and after exchanging pleasantries asked where were
we? I told them Paddington. "That's our area," Deborah said.
"What street are you in?" she asked. I looked around and saw
a street sign. Praed Street. "That's our street," Debby said.
"We're in number 15." Number 15 turned out to be exactly
across the street from where we were standing, and Debby
and Dave were watching us from their bedroom window.

Despite auspicious beginnings, Britain soon struck
me as a nation of disasters. Whereas in New Zealand we would

have a five-car pile-up on the Auckland motorway, in Britain it would be a fifty-car pile-up. And while a train crash would injure one person and maybe kill a cow, in Britain the death toll would be dozens.

The first big story I covered in the UK was the Clapham train crash. It happened on the morning of December 13, 1988, when faulty signals allowed a morning commuter train to ram another, stationary, commuter train. And then, with survivors climbing out onto the tracks, a third train came past and collected them. A fourth train stopped with only metres to spare.

It was a scene of utter carnage, and the first big disaster I'd seen. Within a month I was reporting on an airliner smashing onto the M1 motorway. Three months later, in April, 95 people were crushed to death on the terraces at Hillsborough soccer stadium.

Four months after that, in August, I was standing on the banks of the Thames watching bodies being pulled out of the sunken pleasure boat *Marchioness*. That first year was a heck of an introduction to the job of being a foreign correspondent and, for a while, had me believing I was living in a permanent disaster zone.

But it was the worst one of all, the Lockerbie bombing of December 22, 1988, that I remember most. On December 22 my wife and I were flying to the United States to spend Christmas with her family. We had the choice of flying United Airlines, leaving at around 6.30pm, or of taking Pan Am flight 109 leaving a couple of hours later. We chose United.

We knew nothing of what had happened until we arrived at my in-laws in Florida and turned on the television to see the scenes at New York's Kennedy Airport where people were waiting for the flight that never arrived.

They have a name for the elderly, superannuated gentlemen one finds employed as attendants at clubs and offices around England, in particular at Lord's cricket ground. They're called "jobsworths" as in "I can't let you in there Guv'nor. It's more than my jobsworth."

The worst I ever met was at Lord's one afternoon when I went along, with dozens of other journalists, to cover a press conference to announce the reinstatement of South Africa into world cricket. One jobsworth had directed about 30 of us to the east side of the Long Room, while another jobsworth had directed other journalists to the western door.

The group I was with arrived to find yet a third jobsworth standing before the closed doors refusing us admittance. "You can't go in there," he said. "There's a press conference going on."

"We know," we replied. "We're here to cover it. So just let us in please."

"Sorry. I can't do that. Only journalists are allowed in there."

"But we are journalists."

"How do I know that?"

"By these bloody cameras you old git," someone called out.

Well that was a red rag to a bull, to call a jobsworth a git. The old codger stood his ground and would not allow us past, no way, no how. For about two or three minutes we raged at this man who demanded identification, yet still refused entry, while all the time one of cricket's more important stories was going on inside. Eventually such a noise was being made that a cricket board executive came to the door to see what was going on.

Jobsworth proudly told him he had stopped us interrupting the press conference. "Can't you see they're journalists, you fool," was his reply, and he flung open the doors to let us all in. It taught me a valuable lesson. Never try to reason with a jobsworth.

The BBC really knew how to make a person feel inadequate. The first time I did a standup in front of the Houses of Parliament it was alongside a BBC television crew. My cameraman and I arrived in our car, hassled around and found a park (on a tow-away zone). We unloaded our gear – camera, tripod, batteries, light stand and bag for our microphones. Sharing the gear between us, we trooped off across the grass, found a location, set up and I read off my spiel. All very straightforward.

Then we watched in amazement as our BBC colleagues showed us how it was done. They parked their van in a media-reserved park. Then the parliamentary correspondent walked across the lawn followed by the director carrying a clipboard, a man carrying a light, another carrying the sound gear, another carrying the camera and tripod, and yet another carrying nothing at all.

The correspondent stood on his spot while the director told him what he was going to say. The man with the tripod set that up, as did the man with the light. The soundman prepared the microphone while the camera was put on the stand. When it was finally framed up the man with nothing to do stepped forward, looked through the viewfinder, fiddled a bit with the focus and, on cue, pushed the on button.

When the 10-second piece was finished, it all happened in reverse and the troop of six made their way back to the van.

My cameraman and I then picked up our gear between us and went back to the car. All I could think was, "If only all those people who moan about the licence fee in New Zealand could see this, they'd really have something to complain about." To be fair to the BBC, it has certainly slimmed down since that day in 1989. It sure needed to.

Irish humour is legendary, especially when it's at the expense of one's good self. I was in the southern Irish city of Cork trying to find the local television station. It was a little out of town, and I was quite lost. I came to some cross-roads and stopped and asked a farmer if he could tell me the way to RTE.

"Well," he said, "you're not from around these parts are you?"

"No," I said.

"So you'll be lost then?"

"Yep."

"OK. If you go straight ahead, turn left at the first

intersection, go on for about a mile, you'll come to a pub on the left hand side. That's not RTE, but you can get a good pint of Guinness there. Ha ha ha."

"Ha ha." (Very funny. I was in a bit of a hurry.)

"OK then. If you go right here and up to the lights, on a couple of streets and take the first on the right, you'll still be lost, b'cos it ain't there either. Ha ha ha ha."

(Ha bloody ha with a fixed smile.)

"But if you slowly turn your head to the left you'll see a tall mast, and that, I believe, is RTE. Bye bye." And off he went, straight ahead, turned left at the first intersection . . . and on for a mile, no doubt, to the pub to tell his mates about the latest foreign victim of the legendary Irish wit.

If ever the former British Prime Minister, Margaret Thatcher, made a blunder, it was to force through the poll tax. With this amazing piece of legislation, home-owners no longer paid local-body rates. Instead, everybody over the age of 18 had to. It meant that people who rented properties (the vast majority) had to pay, in some cases, up to £700 per person, per year. Mum, dad, and all the kids. Each had to pay.

In one story I featured an old recluse living in a caravan in a field who was being charged £400 a year poll tax, despite having no road, no power, no sewerage, no nothing. Another was about a pub where the county boundary ran down the middle of the building and through the marital bed. The publican slept in one county, and was charged its tax, while his wife slept in another, and was charged a different sum.

There were all sorts of rumblings in the months leading up to the introduction of the poll tax, mostly at council meetings when the rates were set. In Nottingham City, protesters dressed up as Robin Hood and his merry men and took over the chambers while outside a crowd burnt an effigy of Mrs Thatcher. The poll tax revolt had begun, and rumbled on for the month of March until, on April 1, London erupted.

It began in Trafalgar Square with a huge rally that quickly turned ugly. The police charged the crowd with horses, the crowd fought back and then began to riot. I heard about it and rushed into the office to meet the crew. Because our office was just off Oxford Circus we only had to walk round the corner to be in the thick of it.

It was as though the fun-loving West End had gone crazy. The crowd, mostly young people and many in typical punk clothing (black, with holes), were smashing windows and looting what they liked, setting fires in rubbish bins, turning over cars and beating up the occupants, and fighting with police. The city had gone mad.

I had made the mistake of wearing a jacket and tie. After all, a television reporter must always look neat. Bad move. Collars and ties were a target in the West End that afternoon, and at one stage the people around me started to become quite threatening as I began a standup before the camera. They assumed I must have been a British reporter judging by comments like "Bloody lackey of the capitalists. You bastards are all on the side of the government."

My crew and I had to find refuge among the beleaguered police who were trying to herd the rioters along Oxford Street and Tottenham Court Road. In all the places I had been before, and have been since, it was the only time I have been singled out. Believe me, it was not a nice feeling.

The trouble eventually petered out the further away we got, until eventually the crowd dispersed and we all went home, utterly shocked by the violence. So was Britain. Margaret Thatcher was dumped eight months later. Within four months, so was the poll tax.

Surely few fathers have embarrassed themselves more than I did one week after my daughter Sophie was born on July 18, 1991.

I was sent to cover a concert in Leicester Square featuring Midge Marsden, Dave McCartney, Dianne Swan and other expatriate or visiting New Zealand musicians.

They'd decided to hold a concert for the thousands of young New Zealanders in London at the time. I went to the rehearsal and thoroughly enjoyed meeting musicians I had always admired. In just a few hours of practice they pulled together an entire repertoire guaranteed to get the place rocking.

I was full of the joys of new fatherhood and bored everyone within earshot about the birth. Seeking to impress the musicians, I mentioned how Carol and I had played lots of music to Sophie while she was still in the womb. "Any song in particular?" asked Midge Marsden.

I told him Bob Marley's *Walk and Don't Look Back* was quite a favourite. That night I returned with my cameraman to film the concert. The theatre was packed with young New Zealanders ready for a night of Kiwiana. It was a rocking good concert.

Then, near the end, Midge Marsden announced, "We have a special guest tonight. His wife has just had a beautiful baby daughter. You may know Liam Jeory as TVNZ's London correspondent. He's going to come up here and sing *Walk and Don't Look Back* with us. Come on up Liam."

I was shell-shocked. But in front of 3000 New Zealanders I couldn't refuse for long, and was pushed onto the stage by my cameraman, who was in on the whole thing. Midge saved me by whispering in my ear that I could just help with the chorus and he'd see me through the rest. So I got to sing. And one day, when I want my daughter to know just how much I love her, I'll tell her how far I was prepared to embarrass myself for her when she was just one week old.

The Windsors

Cameron Bennett

On a slow Sunday in London, on a dry week when the grey suits of Westminster were about as exciting as it got, Britain's racy tabloid press exploded with yet another revelation about the hapless House of Windsor. That was my cue to jump.

The "serious" broadsheet papers reluctantly jumped too; tut-tutting about invasions of Royal privacy, and yet reporting the tittle-tattle just the same. It added up to a three-year field day for me; the salacious goings on were relentless. There were Squidgygate and Camillagate; there were Prince Charles' confessions of infidelity and there were allegations of Princess Diana's by way of her former riding instructor. There was talk of the Queen and Prince Philip's "loveless" marriage, of Diana's bulimia, of Charles' indifference towards his children; there was the fire at Windsor in November 1992; Fergie pictured toe-sucking her "financial adviser" in the south of France; even Kiwi gym owner Bryce Taylor got in on the act with covert shots of Di working out.

News editors from Auckland to Toronto and across Western Europe couldn't get enough of it. In my London stint, I watched the House of Windsor stripped of its mystique; reduced, by its own antics, to a figure of ridicule and mockery. But more damaging: this, the apex of the British Establishment, had like never before brought into question the institution of Royalty itself.

Foreign Correspondents

I joined the "Royal Ratpack" on a number of occasions at stakeouts. The "ratpack" is the nickname given to the battery of hard-nosed photographers and hacks who make their livelihoods out of covering every Royal move. The right picture of Diana is worth a small fortune, which means the woman is never safe from the long lens of the society snapper. They come with step ladders and even, on one occasion, scaffolding to build a platform from which they could peer over a sports ground wall at Diana and the two princes.

The ratpack is universally despised, yet their pictures and exposes ensure enormous boosts to newspaper circulations. Royal scuttlebutt sells, but no-one admits buying it.

I experienced the depth of that public loathing on a stakeout outside a house in Fulham, London. It was the home of one of Diana's friends who'd been identified as the source of yet another Diana story in the press. Neighbours walked by within earshot, telling their children that we were the "lowest of the low; nasty scavengers". You can be sure those same neighbours were fully briefed on all the dirt, because they too had gone out and bought the papers.

Despite the Waleses' protestations over invasion of privacy, it was interesting to discover – by way of yet more exposes – to what lengths Charles and Diana would go to manipulate the press to their own ends. That was the reason I was standing outside that house in Fulham and suffering the neighbours' scorn; the woman who lived there had been used to channel Diana's side of the story to the media.

Apart from peering out of a press pen – one of those cordoned-off areas for the media at Royal occasions – the closest I ever got to the Windsor family was a face-to-face interview with Prince Philip. The interview was included in a documentary on Sir Edmund Hillary produced by Mark Sainsbury in New Zealand.

At the time, Buckingham Palace was one of those places you only got to see from the outside; unless you were a dignitary or summoned to be invested with a Royal gong. It was only later that 18 of its 600 rooms would be opened to the public; the Queen needed the money to help pay for restoration of fire damage at Windsor Castle.

The Windsors

A Kiwi, Merv Dunne from the Bay of Islands, was one of the first through the doors. He'd built a bivouac in St James' Park in preparation and became something of a cause celebre. The famous gentlemen's outfitters Moss Bros decked him out in top hat and tails for the big day. I covered the whole hilarious exercise in a feature for *Holmes,* although I'd already had a sneak preview of the palace during a press open day. It was grand but in a garish sort of way; the Green, Blue and White drawing rooms appeared overly ornate with their gilded cornices and sculpted wall panels and reliefs. There was not much homely about the place, apart from some 1950s or '60s era single-bar heaters installed in the fireplaces; the same sort of heaters you'd see in pensioner flats. Of course, the Queen's private quarters were off-limits, along with most of the palace. There were dozens of paintings on display, though just a hint of the Royal collection; it comprises some 10,000 pictures. In many ways, what we got to see resembled a big emporium, but without the grace of some of the great state rooms open to the public in Europe. I remember thinking at the time how outrageous it was that this repository of art and artifacts had not been opened before to the British public; after all, their taxes were keeping Royalty afloat.

But, before that particular foray and before the hoi polloi had been permitted to traipse through the great corridors, I'd been issued with my invitation for an audience with Prince Philip.

Our car was waved in by police officers, and through the gates, past the tourists clinging to the fence and across the crunchy, brown gravel we swept. The crew was awkwardly squeezed into sports jackets and ties; in my experience, TV crews have an aversion to both. I was feeling just as awkward; the Queen's consort was well known for his aversion to the media. But this interview was about Sir Edmund Hillary; we were on safe ground.

Down the corridors adorned with enormous paintings of soldiers, coronations and other regal occasions we went; finally escorted by the Prince's secretary into a small library. The secretary, whose name I can't recall, was the epitome of etiquette and civility. We discussed the form of the proceedings and concluded with the vexed business of how one should address His Royal Highness. Should it be "Prince Philip"? "Sir"? "Your Highness . . ." Before I had established what was polite form, the man himself arrived in the room.

The face was almost as familiar as my father's. Since childhood I'd seen him in newsreels and magazines: Prince Philip in naval uniform, Prince Philip in a business suit pronouncing on wildlife or commerce, Prince Philip with hands clasped behind his back walking one step behind the Queen on their endless circumnavigations of the Commonwealth, Prince Philip . . . and here I was in his personal library for a one-on-one conversation. Though an old man by then, he still cut an erect and imperious figure, exuding the confidence that goes with absolute authority. That and his legendary unwillingness to suffer fools lightly was very much apparent.

In the flurry of it all, the question of honorifics was lost. What did his equerry say again? My mind was blank. The Prince settled on calling me "you", even though I had been introduced by name. That settled my dilemma: I called him "you" too. Ours was to be a conversation between two "yous".

I'd presumed Prince Philip knew more about Sir Edmund Hillary than he actually did, given that Sir Edmund's triumph over Mount Everest coincided with the Coronation in 1953. Prince Philip said he did not know Sir Edmund particularly well, so our conversation was more about the significance of the great climber's achievements.

Near the end of what would have been a 20-minute audience, I recall asking HRH whether we could return to a point he had made earlier, in the interests of accuracy. He quipped, sarcastically, that that would have to be a first for someone from the news media. Given the wringer his family had been put through, I suppose his remark wasn't surprising.

And then it was all over; my one and only interview with Royalty at an end. As we were packing up the lighting kit and audio equipment, my cameraman, Richard Malone, asked whether the sound recordist or myself had noticed HRH's tie pin. We hadn't, but Malone had. The Royal tie was apparently secured to the Royal shirt by way of a safety pin – an enamel-headed nappy pin, no less. Malone, to this day, insists the nappy pin was even a little rusty.

The London Beat

Cameron Bennett

"No, Sir, when a man is tired of London," wrote Dr Samuel Johnson, "he is tired of life . . ." It's always been that sort of town for me: frustrating, yes; wearying, often; boring, never. As TVNZ's "man in London", that city with all its diversity, hilarity, history and solemnity was wide open, like Britain itself.

When I returned in October 1991, it was like putting on a pair of comfortable old shoes. It fitted; it felt familiar. I'd learnt its main routes as a van driver in the early 1980s. I'd dealt with its bureaucratic pedantry before as a freelance print journalist and office clerk.

Almost a decade later, I was back as a paid observer looking from the outside in on anything from the peculiar eccentricities of the British Establishment to the peculiar eccentricities of English train spotters. There was nothing predictable about the job or the hours I worked. While Auckland may have been working Monday to Friday, London never did; IRA bombers often saw to that, or yet another Royal crisis.

As TVNZ's Europe Correspondent, the job always came first. That meant an unusual strain on my family. In the first 10 months of 1994, for instance, I was away for four of them. I became somewhat of a stranger to my two young sons,

Foreign Correspondents

Angus and Calum. So much so, that recently Angus announced that when he grew up he'd have a job which didn't take him away from home. Phyl, my wife, is often asked how she coped. She says that for all the hardship, the separation, the single parenting, she wouldn't have missed it for anything. She, too, had lived in London before; she did not feel alienated by it. On the contrary, she relished what the town had to offer. From my viewpoint, the posting could never have worked without her support. She had to face the prospect of my visits to war zones, and the very real chance that I might not come back in one piece. She never stinted.

So taken were we both with the posting that, although tired after three years, we were extremely reluctant to give it up.

For a journalist, London is the pinnacle of the English-speaking world. Years earlier, I'd padded my way up and down Fleet Street, soaking it all in; the famous newspaper titles and the almost as famous newspaper pubs. I dreamt of a job on one of those big-name papers. To be back, as a fully-fledged foreign correspondent in 1991; to be recording sign-off standups in front of the Houses of Parliament, was a thrill I never lost.

There weren't any other foreign bureaux in London quite like ours that I came across. I was called a Europe Correspondent but my footprint extended well outside Europe; to the east coast of the United States, where I covered the election of President Clinton, to Africa and Russia. My bureau colleagues and I used Heathrow Airport like other people would use a taxi rank. Our crews were almost permanently on the road.

In one epic voyage with Prime Minister Jim Bolger in early 1993, we travelled from London to Dublin, back to London, up to Edinburgh, across to Belfast, south to County Wexford, across to Brussels, on to Warsaw and finally Moscow.

There can be few other jobs that offer such access. I have toured the halls of Number 10 Downing Street and the Kremlin, been into the highly-secure palace of the King and

Queen of Spain and Buckingham Palace, seen the Stasi secret police headquarters in what was East Berlin, rubbed shoulders with some of the most powerful figures in Europe.

There can be few other jobs, either, that offer such variety. On one day you could be covering the latest crisis to rock John Major's cabinet, the next, in suburban Croydon, where people are upset by a neighbour's decision to mount an enormous fibreglass marlin on the roof of his house. There were stories of the national conker championship. That's when grown English men tie chestnuts to pieces of string and swat at their opponent's conker. The first one to split the other's conker wins, and much merry morris dancing follows. There were the hardy annuals of Brits coping badly with soaring summer temperatures, all deck-chairs and perspiration in the overcrowded tubes; the Queen Mother, incredibly, notching up yet another birthday. Or there could be Kiri Te Kanawa wowing the opera buffs; the insurmountable problems many Brits face over joining Europe; the "Loo of the Year" award, and the chap who works in a kilt shop in Edinburgh and goes by the name of Prince Michael of Albany, the rightful heir to Bonnie Prince Charlie's throne. It never stops.

For me, there was always a certain bemusement over some of the locations I found myself in, particularly in Britain; like Harrod's, where, years before, I'd been a hamper-packer and the garden gnome salesman, or doing business as a client of Worldwide Television News, the foreign news agency where I got my start in television as scriptwriter.

My last assignment out of the UK, in late 1994, was an appropriate one for putting out the old and bringing in the new. It was a media tour on the inaugural train trip from Waterloo Station to Brussels through the newly opened Channel Tunnel.

History was in the making; Britain, like it or not, was now tethered to Europe, and it seemed that every free-loading hack was determined to be there to mark the occasion. In a gesture of rash exuberance, the organisers provided generous refreshments for the entire return journey. Emotions flared; at least one Englishman on board was determined that, tunnel or not, Britain was still very much an island.

He led the charge at the customs post in Brussels. When asked for identification, he shouted that this was discrimination against Brits and if they called this European union then forget it. On the trip home, and the worse for wear, our man again took the floor, pronouncing loudly on the shortfalls of his European neighbours, while quietly taking a seat in first class that had been reserved for a visiting Japanese. On being asked by the mild-mannered Japanese if there had been some mistake, our Englishman – still smarting over the loss of Fortress Britain – retorted, "Thinking of buying it are we? Buying the whole bloody train are we? Bought every-bloody-thing else!"

Fast Track to Washington

Liam Jeory

It was 1am when the call from Auckland woke me up –
"How quickly can you get to Washington?"

Not only was I the European Correspondent, I was also the northern hemisphere correspondent. Television New Zealand had just been informed that the Minister of Foreign Affairs and Trade, Mike Moore, was about to meet the US Secretary of State, James Baker. We had to be there to record the historic thaw in New Zealand's relationship with the United States, frozen for the previous six years over New Zealand's anti-nuclear stance. From London, I was closer than anyone else. No ifs and buts, I just had to be there.

No great difficulty, you may think, except that the meeting was taking place in just 10 hours' time.

As a foreign correspondent, I always had a current US visa in my passport, which was one potential difficulty out of the way. The second was how to get there in time. British Airways said there was only one way – take the Concorde. Now Concorde is not cheap. It costs as much as a first class ticket, and then some. So at 1.20am I was busy telling my editor that if he really wanted the story, I'd just have to catch the next Concorde to New York, much as it would pain me to have to take such a flight. As I recall, the answer was "Humph!

Well you can go there on Concorde but you're damn well going home economy."

Next I rang the Washington DC office of Worldwide Television News to arrange a cameraman to be waiting for me at the State Department. It was easier to use an American cameraman (who already had the security clearances to operate in federal buildings) than to take my own. Having been forced to spring for one Concorde flight, the TVNZ budget wasn't going to stretch to two.

I got no more sleep that night. There were shirts to iron and clothes to pack, into the office for my computer and some research material, then the hour-long taxi ride to the airport.

I felt a bit out of place in the BA Concorde lounge at half past five in the morning. Only the richest, grandest, highest-flying take the Concorde. None of them have to iron their own shirts, I'll bet. I'd been told that on Concorde flights you'll always see someone famous. On my flight it was the American crooner Willie Nelson.

On to the plane itself. What struck me was how small it was; only two seats, a narrow aisle, then two more seats in width. And they weren't huge, luxurious, first class seats with built-in everything. They were small, blue, leather-covered seats, and snug. Now I like planes, speed, G-forces – the lot. All I really wanted was for the pilot to open this baby up so I could experience life at two and a half times the speed of sound. But, like so many things in life, expectation and reality are two different things.

The pilot no sooner took off in a crescendo of noise and acceleration than he throttled back. By law Concorde can't break the speed of sound until it's out over the Bristol Channel. It was a very normal flight for the first 15 minutes or so but once over the ocean the pilot let her rip. There wasn't much sensation within the aircraft itself but I was watching a digital readout on the bulkhead which told us as we passed the sound barrier, then on to almost two and a half times the speed of sound. The only sensation was a slight lurch as we went through the sound barrier, much like a car with an automatic gearbox as it goes from gear to gear.

The only other thing of note is that we flew almost twice as high as a normal jet aircraft – up where the sky begins to change colour to a very deep blue, and from where the ground below is almost out of sight. A jumbo jet flying below us looked about the size of a very small sparrow.

Concorde is a first class flight; there's no such thing as economy on this plane. I'd been awake for some six hours by now and was really starving. But there was no chance of bacon and eggs, a bit of toast and a piping hot coffee. Oh no. On Concorde they started with caviar and salmon titbits, a leaf of exotic lettuce, followed by eggs – quail eggs – and finished off with a light mousse and demitasse coffee. I landed in New York some two and a half hours after leaving London, exhilarated but starving.

So much for the glamour of Concorde. Now I came down to earth with a thump. My connecting flight was a small commuter plane from New York to Washington DC. Again, it was the only flight that could get me there in time. Unfortunately, it was the proverbial "flight from hell". The air conditioning had broken down, and hot air was being pumped into the cabin all the way to Washington. The flight crew were aware of it, but unable to do anything to stop it. As the temperature rose into the mid thirties, we were all sweating profusely, taking off our ties and jackets and gulping down cold drinks as fast as the attendant could serve them. About half an hour into the flight the plane got its first victim, an elderly woman who fainted, followed by other people complaining of nausea.

We got down on the ground not a moment too soon. I was soaking wet, smelling like a polecat and with a headache to end all headaches. But I couldn't do anything about it. I had less than an hour to catch a taxi to the State Department, meet my cameraman, get through security and up to the photo call to record a public handshake between Mike Moore and James Baker. The old "one picture tells a thousand words" argument – that's what this whole thing was about.

There I was, standing behind a rope barrier with other

camera crews and reporters, having been briefed endlessly that "the secretary will not be taking questions", when my cameraman collapsed. Two minutes to the scheduled photo call, thousands of dollars already spent to ensure the moment was caught on film, and my cameraman was out cold. I thought he'd had a heart attack and started poking around in his mouth looking for his tongue, trying to remember whether or not to begin heart massage. Luckily he started to stir before I had to do anything.

"My pills. In my pocket. Pills." It seems he had a nervous disorder, something he kept under control by medication. In the rush of the morning, he'd forgotten to take them. In the confusion we'd quite forgotten about Moore and Baker. As the doors started to open, I was truly caught between a rock and a hard place. I'd raced all the way from London for this very moment and now we weren't ready. What would my excuse be for not getting the story? Did I continue to administer to my cameraman and forget about the two politicians? Or did I pick up the camera and try to shoot it myself? I pose the questions because, mercifully, I never had to answer them. From his position on the floor, my cameraman was insistent that he could do it.

So I hoisted the heavy camera onto his shoulder and stood behind helping prop him up while Messrs Moore and Baker stepped out, shook hands and left. My cameraman promptly collapsed again. So did I, almost.

The rest of the day was a breeze. A press conference at the New Zealand embassy. An interview with the US Assistant Secretary of State. Back to the WTN offices to edit the story. Nothing to it. Satellite the story home – done it a million times. I was walking on air (although, remembering that sweaty little plane trip, pretty foul air I must say). Time to find somewhere to stay. In all the rush I'd quite forgotten to book a hotel. But after all I'd been through, that wouldn't be a problem, would it?

It was getting pretty late when I walked over the road to the nearest hotel. No, they didn't have a room. Please? No, they still didn't have a room. The place was fully booked out.

Fast Track to Washington

Did they have a broom closet then? Just a joke. Actually, they did. They'd just redecorated a former closet (albeit a huge closet) as a small overnight room for people in a hurry, and if I didn't mind the paint fumes they would prepare that for me. By now I was so stuffed, so hungry and so needing a shower I couldn't be bothered looking any further. I spent the night in Washington DC in, literally, a broom cupboard.

What occurred the next morning belongs in the realm of urban myth. Everyone knows a "friend's father's brother" who it happened to. And now to Liam Jeory. I'd ordered a newspaper and went to my closet door to get it. The maid, or whoever had delivered it, had placed it in the passageway tantalisingly out of immediate reach. Being about to step into the shower I was naked but, with no-one in sight, I figured I could just get it. Almost. With a bit of a stretch. If I just kept my foot in the door and really leant out, I could get it.

Well, I shouldn't have tried. The door closed and I was stuck in the corridor, buck naked and with no key to get back inside. I really couldn't believe it happened to me. Neither could the couple who stepped out of their room moments later. They promised to call a bellhop to bring up a key, and no, they didn't think I was weird to be standing naked in the corridor. There was nothing left for me to do but to sit down, arrange the classified ads to provide a modicum of decency, nod hello to various people as they passed me by on their way down to breakfast, and catch up on the news.

I was pretty well read by the time the young bellhop arrived with a key. When he looked at me a little strangely, I told him that when he'd been in the job a little longer he'd get to see a whole lot worse.

I was married just outside Washington DC in 1984, and over the years had visited it many times. So the city is no stranger to me. It's never hard to fill in time waiting for a flight in a city that boasts the Smithsonian Museum. After all the rush getting here, the trip home was going to be positively leisurely. In fact it was so leisurely that when I reported for my return flight it was overbooked. I was given two choices. I could either wait around on standby and hope that someone didn't turn up or I could take $US500, spend the night at an airport hotel and catch the early morning flight. I took the money.

Now here's where the circle becomes complete. The early flight to New York was uneventful; the air conditioning worked. But as I was waiting for the connecting flight across the Atlantic, a flight attendant came up to the six of us who'd been bumped the previous night to say that Concorde was leaving in half an hour with three spare seats on board. British Airways would like to make up for our inconvenience, and was going to draw our names from a hat. All five. All except me. I was excluded because I'd already flown on Concorde.

THE THIRD WORLD WAR – ALMOST

Fun and Games in the Gulf War

Liam Jeory

I was sitting at home watching television when the news came through that Iraq had invaded Kuwait. I can distinctly remember thinking that after all I had been through in the previous year, I was going to top it off with a war.

There was never any doubt that I was going to the Gulf, the big question was where? Kuwait would have been the obvious place, but the Iraqis weren't giving out visas in those early days – they were too busy looting and conquering. Saudi Arabia was right next door, and making belligerent noises; but trying to get a visa for there was harder than breaking into the Queen's bedroom at Buckingham Palace.

Jordan was the obvious place to go because, as it was friendly with Iraq, its border was still open. And it was over that border that trapped Westerners were escaping, including a number of New Zealanders. It was a strange time in those early days of the Gulf War, full of military experts filling our heads with tales of the doomsday weapons of Saddam Hussein.

There was his nuclear programme and whether he had the bomb. More importantly, was he mad enough to use it? There were his chemical and biological weapons, which he had already used on the Kurds. And he had his Scud missiles with enough range to hit Israel. All of a sudden the idea of going to Jordan, smack bang between Iraq and its deadly enemy, Israel, lost its appeal. If we went we had to be prepared.

The hottest item in London in those early days were chemical warfare suits. The army had lightweight suits that looked like army fatigues with layers of carbon between the lining, form fitting gas masks – stuff designed for the 1990s. But us? One of my Aussie colleagues managed to track down a heavy rubber job that looked something like an orchardist's spray suit, with heavy gumboots and a hood that looked like a beekeeper's helmet. It must have been designed and built in the 1950s, and it was all that journalists could lay their hands on.

The military experts were telling us that Iraqi chemical weapons could kill in less than two minutes. So that was how long we had to get into these suits if we were to have any chance of survival. Fat chance. The best any of us managed was around five minutes. Iraq would have completed an entire invasion by the time we were into the suit. We concluded it was a complete waste of time. If we were going to war, we'd just have to take our chances.

So off we trooped down to the Jordanian embassy, Rob, Michael, Paul, Ross, Drew and I – the Anzacs off to war. We made our applications to an extremely friendly Jordanian press attaché, whose job it was to vet all applications by journalists wanting to visit his country.

It turns out he'd worked in Canberra some years before, and was very kindly disposed towards Australians and New Zealanders. Not that a bunch of British photographers who applied at the same time were to know. There must have been a dozen of them, hunting together, which is why they're known as the ratpack. They're friendly in a hale and hearty sort of way but are universally loathed by their prey, philandering politicians and topless Royals.

After a wait of about an hour, ours were the first names called to receive our visas. That raised a howl of protest from the waiting Brits. "We was here first. How come you're getting yours before us. Where's you from anyway?"

As we picked up our visas, the press attaché confided in us. "I can't stand those guys. They think they can bully me. You guys are OK. But them? I'm going to keep them waiting for days."

"See you in Jordan," the ratpackers called as we left.

They did make it, but not for some time. We'd been in Amman for three days, filed numerous stories, a couple of live interviews with Richard Long and Judy Bailey, and attended a major rally by the time they arrived in town. We were relaxing by the pool in the early evening sun when we heard them coming. The banter went something like this:

"Gawd, that was a long flight. I need a rest."

"Me too. And a drink."

"Yeah. A good pint of bitter."

"A pint of bitter? A pint of bitter? 'Ere we are in exotic Jordan and you want to order a pint of bitter. You bloody cretin. What about some sort of cocktail or summit?"

"Orright then." And he called over the waiter. "Oi! Garcon. How about a pint of your most exotic cocktail then?"

There was a sort of carnival atmosphere in Amman in those days. The world's media had descended on the place and taken over the International Hotel. During the day we'd roam the city looking for stories and at night we'd gather in the bar and catch up with people I'd last seen in South Africa, Berlin, Prague or Bucharest. It was like a foreign correspondents' reunion.

And it was like a phony war, full of posturing by Saddam Hussein and the Western leaders ranged against him. Jordan was squarely behind the Iraqi leader, seeing him as standing up to the West. It was incredibly easy to stir an angry crowd. All we had to do was set up a camera and people would gather round. It mattered not that I was a New Zealander and my crew Australian. As far as they were concerned we looked like Americans, or sounded British, and that was just as bad. They never attacked us physically but would get so carried away with their denunciations of the West that we would invariably have to make good our escape before the threats turned to violence. Any businesses with a Western name were taking down their signs to avoid trouble.

We had a hint of the Jordanians' paranoia within minutes of touching down in Amman for the first time. The sun was starting to set and we wanted to do a standup to show that we had arrived. So as soon as we stepped outside the terminal we pulled out the camera and I proceeded to do a report in front of the airport building, something along the lines of "this airport is bound to become a centre of attention as Western hostages start to arrive from Iraq looking to get home".

I hadn't even finished before the airport police pounced and hauled us away. They held us for a couple of hours before they were satisfied that we weren't spies. We had been warned that Jordan was more than a little twitchy.

A few days later Rob and I decided to go for a drive along the main road to Baghdad; along the road that refugees were escaping out of Iraq and Jordanian lorries were carrying supplies in defiance of the United Nations sanctions. We stopped some 30 kilometres out of Amman, at a point chosen at random, to film the road, the traffic, and do our standups.

We had barely started filming when a battered little ute driven by an elderly Jordanian in a flowing gown and headgear pulled up. Then he took off at high speed to return some minutes later with a police car. We were under arrest. Unbeknown to us, we had stopped in a restricted military area. Just behind a low hill next to the road, and completely out of our sight, was the main Jordanian Army tank park.

We were taken back to the local police station, to be ushered into the office of the police chief. It was all slightly unreal. The chief looked like a Mexican bandit. He wasn't exactly friendly, thinking he had caught four spies in the act. To add insult, in a pair of swim trunks I wasn't exactly dressed for the occasion. I had a nice shirt on, which is all I needed when the viewers were only going to see my head and shoulders. Still, although it was thirty-plus degrees, a pair of short shorts weren't exactly the clothes to wear in public in this Middle Eastern country, especially when the interrogation was about to begin.

He demanded to know what we were doing. So we told him, and offered him our tape to prove it. We were only filming the road, some traffic, and me talking to the camera. Big mistake. At the top of the tape Drew had shot a particularly beautiful young lady swimming in the hotel pool, paying particular attention to her assets. It was this the police chief first saw when we rewound the tape. I don't know whether it was a smart move or not, but the chief demanded to see the tape again, and again.

After that he relaxed, smiled and offered us tea. Little were we to know that this was the beginning of a long and unique Jordanian torture. We told our story again, looked at the tape a couple of times, had more tea, more talk, and more tea. Soon we had to go to the toilet; a Jordanian police cell toilet. A non-flushing full to the brim hole in the ground. Let me tell you, that was the torture.

By the time we got back to the chief's office he'd been joined by two plainclothes "friends".

Back to the movie script. One was tall, dark, sullen, and wearing sunglasses . . . inside the office. The other was short, tubby, very friendly, and wearing sunglasses also – 007 and Maxwell Smart had arrived. They heard our story, looked at the tape, offered us more tea and saw us back off to the toilet. No matter what they said they never gave us any indication that they believed us when we said it was all an honest mistake.

Finally the chief said we were being moved to another station, for "just a few more questions". It turned out to be the regional headquarters, and we were the centre of attention, guarded by what must have been at least 30 policemen while upstairs the chiefs looked over our tape, again, and again, while we drank more tea. It seemed rude to refuse.

We were allowed a phone call back to our hotel, which is how the message that I was under detention got to London and from there to Television New Zealand. By now we'd been held for some six hours, and still there was no sign of letting us go. Either the police still thought we were spies, and our standups were a secret code, or Drew's soft porn pictures had them hooked.

Finally, after we'd been held for about eight hours, the police decided to let us go, and passed us over to the army. We were taken to some barracks at yet another town and ushered into the office of the military intelligence chief. He knew we weren't spies, but wasn't prepared to let us go without a lecture on the dangers of filming in a prohibited area and of wearing swim trunks in public. We promised never to do it again, and left somewhat chastened by the whole experience. But not Drew. He continued to film pretty women wherever he went.

Back in London as the hostage drama developed and momentum grew towards a military solution, Television New Zealand had to make a decision how to cover such a huge event. I was the only correspondent and obviously couldn't be everywhere at once. Also, British reporters went with the British troops, Americans with the Americans and so on. We didn't have a New Zealand presence, at least not early in the piece, and no-one was much interested in having a Kiwi tag along. So we resolved that we would leave the military reporting to those reporters on the ground and I would cover the New Zealand angle, whenever and wherever Kiwis were involved. That left plenty to do.

Among the hostages trapped in Iraq and Kuwait, held as bargaining chips by Saddam, were several New Zealanders. I can say proudly that I met every single one of them as they were released. I flew to Jordan three times to meet up with New Zealanders released into Jordan and to interview David Lange on his mercy trip to Baghdad. But mostly I met the Kiwi hostages at Heathrow or Gatwick airports in London.

That entailed waiting behind a rope outside the special reception areas, usually at four or five o'clock in the morning with hundreds of other media, and as the hostages came out trying to identify the Kiwis. One way was to hold up a New Zealand flag. Calling out "Any Kiwis" often did the trick. Or fellow journalists from other countries would help out. "Hey Liam. I've got a couple of your New Zealanders down here."

Fun and Games in the Gulf War

"Thanks Mark. I'll trade you five Aussies up this end."

It was a most undignified way of dealing with people who had harrowing tales to tell, had just completed long journeys, and were now faced with a battery of cameras and lights, being traded around among journalists like booty. It was the last way I wanted to deal with the Tolley family.

Mark Tolley was an Australian whose New Zealand wife, Gaela, and three children were trapped in Kuwait. He had appeared on TVNZ a number of times pleading for diplomatic assistance to get her out. He had begun to hatch all sorts of plans to infiltrate Kuwait, find his wife, and whisk her out through enemy lines. He wasn't a fool, just desperate. And stuck in London without a job, all his money and assets in Kuwait, he was without resources.

Finally news came through that Gaela and the children had been forcibly taken to Iraq and were to be released with the last planeload of women and children to come out. Mark and I got on well, and I offered to drive him out to the airport and bring the family home. Actually I had an ulterior motive as well. Everybody wanted to talk to the Tolleys and I wanted an exclusive. So at four thirty in the morning we drove out to Gatwick together. I drove up to the security entrance, fully intending to drop Mark off, park the car, and join my crew, and competitors, waiting behind the lines.

The guard at the door made the assumption that Mark and I were family, called someone over to park our car, and ushered us both in. He didn't seem to hear some of my competitors calling out "Oi, what's he going in there for. Hey Liam, how are you getting in?" I was thinking that they were going to stuff it up for me good and proper. But the security guard simply made some remark about "watch out for those vultures out there". I mumbled "Yeah. You can't trust them" or something along those lines, and followed Mark. He got me through the subsequent security checks by calling me his "mate". So it was I found myself in the waiting area, chatting to Richard Branson, whose Virgin Airlines was flying out the hostages, and the British Undersecretary for Foreign Affairs.

The reunions were quite something; families coming off the plane to finally be with their loved ones. Mostly it was the relief on their faces that they were really safe. But for the vast majority of the women and children there was a sadness too, because most had to leave their husbands and fathers behind. Saddam was holding them as part of his human shield. Gaela Tolley and her children, Nicholas, Sam and Jesse, were among the happiest of all, because their family was complete.

They entered into the spirit of my secret agent enterprise, ducking into the car without talking to the other media despite calls of "Gaela, love – over here. Just a smile, love, there's a girl." I took off at high speed because, by now, some of the other media had figured what had happened and were trying to follow. The young boys thought it was all great fun. I used the car phone to call New Zealand, and Gaela did a phone interview with our TVNZ late news while I gunned the car up and down the side roads of Surrey trying to shake off any following vehicles. It was Keystone Kops. If only the viewers back home knew what was really going on.

The Tolley family spent the rest of the day together, resting and catching up before I interviewed them, secure now in the knowledge that the rest of the media didn't know where they were. Gaela had a harrowing tale to tell; of how an Iraqi soldier tried to rape her, and, when he failed, went to another house, tied up the husband and had his way. That soldier was later executed. Because she spent a month in Kuwait actually hiding out from the Iraqis, she had to flee from abandoned apartment to apartment, always on the lookout and always trying to dream up ways of getting out. Kuwaitis who may have wanted to help hiding Westerners were threatened with hanging if they were caught. And she described her children's reactions. One boy thought it was exciting at first, then got bored being locked up inside for a month. The next boy became distressed and would never let his mother out of his sight. The youngest just ate constantly.

Four days later I was on my way back into Jordan, to meet up with the crew of an RNZAF Hercules which had flown

Fun and Games in the Gulf War

in with a load of milk powder, and was engaged in flying Pakistani refugees who'd fled Kuwait and Iraq back to Karachi. It was truly effective aid, seeing the milk powder being used to feed thousands of people stuck in the refugee camps that had sprung up around Amman, and seeing hundreds of those refugees being returned home via a New Zealand Air Force plane.

Refugee camps are truly wretched places, with the lucky few living under tents, and the vast majority under plastic sheets, tarpaulins or nothing at all. Jordan simply couldn't cope. As a journalist, I could at least visit, and then go back to eat, sleep and make merry with the rest of the press corps at the International Hotel. It made the RNZAF crew feel a bit guilty as well. Their biggest worry was that, as I interviewed them at their luxury hotel, their friends back home would think they were on a holiday.

There were still seventeen New Zealand hostages in Iraq and Kuwait when David Lange arrived in Jordan in November 1990 on his way to try to organise their release. Other politicians had gone to Baghdad on the same sort of mercy missions before. It was almost a convention of former prime ministers. Edward Heath from Britain, Willy Brandt from Germany, and now David Lange from New Zealand. Lange was the first one to plead specifically for the New Zealanders. I flew to Jordan specially to cover his visit, although the Iraqis still wouldn't grant me a visa to enter their country.

So I interviewed Lange at the end of his flying visit. He told me it helped him enormously that the White House had criticised his going to Baghdad, and while he couldn't announce anything, he strongly advised me not to rush home just yet. That was easier suggested than done. After all the travelling I'd done and all the places I'd been to, this particular trip to Jordan was the first time my luggage had ever gone astray. They didn't find it for four days. So for four days I was reduced somewhat in my wardrobe choice, being a polyester plaid number from the hotel shop and a T-shirt. When I did finally get the call to pick up my bag at Amman airport, I arrived to find it in the middle of the concourse, the zip open and some of the contents strewn around. It is testimony to the honesty of Jordanians, or the quality of my wardrobe, that nothing seemed to be missing.

The enforced layover certainly paid dividends. Within three days, on 15 November, two more New Zealanders were on their way out of Baghdad on an unscheduled flight. Geoff Frost and Barry Lovegrove were free. On the 16th, Ian Mills followed, and on the 17th it was the turn of Michael Wride and Bob Beaton. All were singing the praises of Lange's mercy mission. Bob Beaton had spent all but six nights of his three months as a captive sleeping out in the open air. As he told me, "Then Mr Lange came and, bingo, we were out."

It was now that I was finally granted a visa to go to Baghdad. After months and months of waiting for the application to be processed, the Iraqis finally said yes, and I said no. I had a flight to catch, back to London, because the biggest hostage release of all was about to take place. On the 19th of November all remaining 10 New Zealand hostages were released and flown out from Baghdad. And I kept my one hundred percent record of being there to meet each and every one. With their release my war coverage took a different turn.

I returned to the gulf in February 1991, because by now the shooting had started and New Zealand had committed forces to the Gulf War. They were navy and army medical teams attached to British and American field hospitals in Bahrain. It was significant that they were non-combatants, but were still the first bit of military co-operation between New Zealand and the United States since the Anzus row of the early 'eighties. It was interesting not only to see our forces in the war zone, but also to see how they were getting on. Famously, as it turned out.

The army medical team was based at an American Navy camp which had been shipped from the States in modular form and set up in the middle of the island. An entire hospital in the middle of a desert, surrounded by green tents, some of which housed the New Zealanders. I expected an air of, at worst, hostility, at best, indifference towards the Kiwis.

Fun and Games in the Gulf War

After all, this was a US Navy installation, and it was US Navy visits that had been most affected by New Zealand's anti-nuclear policy. But the first comment from an American to me was, "We're all working as a team, and everybody loves the Kiwis." It wasn't hard to see why.

Everywhere at this massive camp there were signs of the Kiwis. From the sign to Ward Three that said "Kia Ora" to the tourism posters of New Zealand that adorned the hallways of the hospital. The Kiwi soldiers had printed T-shirts that said "Patriot appreciators society" in reference to the American anti-missile missiles. The American soldiers were buying them in droves.

The New Zealand tents really stood out. They were different. They had car pads and barbecue areas set out in concrete, a parade area out front, and a satellite dish out the back. It seems that when the camp was being laid out by the American field engineers, the Kiwis mucked in to help. And when the concrete boxing was laid out for each tent, the New Zealanders, being helpful, laid their own. Which is why they had a car pad, barbecue area and parade ground.

The satellite dish was a bit of Kiwi ingenuity, not to mention cheek. They had told the American soldiers in the tents around them that they had a special Scud alert system to warn them of any impending missile attacks. They'd taken an umbrella, painted it silver, set it up on a microphone stand, and run a lead from it along the ground and inside the tent. In order to demonstrate its use, one of the Kiwi medics would sit out of sight with a radio and simply tune it in and out of the short-wave clutter while others outside moved the antenna, calling out, "Left a little. A little more. That's it. We're locked in." They would then announce there were no missiles on their way, and the American soldiers would wander off secure in the knowledge they were safe for the moment. It must have worked. The base was never attacked. And the Kiwis' gullible neighbours kept asking.

But there was a very serious side to it all. The Royal New Zealand Navy medics, based in another part of Bahrain at a hospital with the British Air Force, brought it home to me.

Their base was next door to the RAF Tornados taking off at all hours, loaded to the hilt with bombs and missiles, and returning some hours later having been all the way into Iraq and back. Some aircraft had already been downed and pilots captured. This was a wartime base, on a war footing.

The great fear was a gas attack and everywhere I went I had a gasmask strapped to my side. The British hospital was completely gas-proof and hidden under huge camouflage nets. To enter I had to go through an air lock and then inside a huge inflated village. There was nothing medical that couldn't be handled in this hospital, although, with no casualties to work on, the only treatment I observed was a tooth being filled.

All the time war was raging, albeit in a one-sided fashion. Peter Arnett from CNN was reporting from inside Baghdad, some reporters filed from among the troops waiting for the ground assault to begin, and the rest sat in Saudi Arabia, hundreds of miles behind the lines, and reported the latest press releases and military briefings from the safety of their hotels.

A few reporters tried to break the rules and go where the military said they couldn't. One TV crew from CBS America were promptly arrested by the Iraqis and spent much of the war in a cell in Baghdad. Initiative was frowned on.

Such is the modern conflict where a reporter can cover a whole war without ever seeing a bullet fired or a dead body; for the vast majority of journalists, without ever being in danger at all. The Gulf War bears no comparison at all with Vietnam or the conflict in Yugoslavia.

So when people say to me, as they do, "The Gulf War, that must have been dangerous?" all I can say is, "It was among the safer of my assignments."

The Road to Baghdad

Cameron Bennett

I saw those first pictures of the Gulf War, with its smart bombs and "surgical" strikes, on a TV set high above the counter of a fish and chip shop in Taupo. I was ordering an extra spring roll at the time. Two years later I was boxing down the desert highway linking Jordan to Iraq, in the back of a GMC V8 jeep; I was on the road to Baghdad.

It was February 1993 and an icy wind cut across the Iraqi sands; the snow had been lying thick beside the roads outside Amman. The distance overland between the Jordanian capital and Baghdad is 1000 kilometres. International sanctions ensured no-one could fly in or out; the only route to this ancient Arabian city was by road.

Since childhood, the name "Baghdad" had conjured up a great sense of mystery and adventure to me. I'd travelled through Morocco and Egypt and lived for a while in Israel, but the "real" Arabia had been off-limits. Now, though, Baghdad had an altogether more sinister ring to it. This was Saddam Hussein's fortress, and despite everything the West had thrown at him, he was still very much in power. From the border post with neighbouring Jordan his all-pervading presence was made felt.

At the time, tension against the West was again running very high. Just a fortnight earlier, the US had fired a number of Tomahawk missiles at targets in Baghdad. My worry was that we would be turned away; the purpose of our visit, after all, included reports on Kiwi servicemen involved in the destruction of Saddam's chemical weapons. It had been a delicate enough business just organising visas in the first place. I had been warned that journalists were having no luck out of the Iraqi embassy in London, and that the way to fast-track a visa was through the Iraqi legation in Jordan. Even then, it was far from certain that an entry permit would be granted.

My telexes to the ambassador in Amman were little short of grovelling; along the lines that viewers in New Zealand were deeply interested in the plight of the Iraqi people in the wake of the Gulf War and that, having faced international ostracism over our anti-nuke policy, New Zealanders would be as receptive as any in the West to Iraq's woes.

It worked. Cameraman Richard Malone and myself were on the first flight out of London before they could change their minds.

In Jordan, the first challenge was to find a vehicle and driver. I'd established by way of calls to the local Reuters agency that this was negotiated at a bus station in Amman. Middle East bus stations, in my experience, have their own special character. They are crowded with people who have sat and waited for who knows how long; there are street vendors, beggars, deafening public address systems, the gritty stench of diesel engine, conductors – three or more to a bus – either touting for customers or shoe-horning yet another passenger into their already over-crowded and dangerously listing buses. Somewhere off to the side of all of this, by the petrol bowsers, were a couple of jeeps available for hire. After the customary haggling over the price, we were on our way.

Our driver spoke not a word of English. We shared moustaches and sign-language in common. A luxuriant moustache is a manly statement in the Arab world, much as it is in West Auckland. Mine apparently met with approval and, I like to think, went some way to allaying local suspicions about our character. As to the character of the driver, it was difficult to tell: there was his flowing moustache, of course, but there was also the remarkable way he'd wired up half a dozen red brake-lights on the inside of the jeep. It lit up like a bordello.

I didn't know what to expect of Iraq. Would it have the broken-down look of a defeated country? Would its infrastructure be intact?

What struck me first was the superb condition of the highway. The contrast couldn't have been more marked after the pot-holed road across Jordan. Then there was Baghdad itself. A modern if slightly sterile city, you could have been forgiven for wondering if bombers had pummelled it at all. The bridges and factories had been rebuilt; there was little to show for the fury of the Gulf War.

But it was a thin veneer; the impact of the Gulf War, and the eight-year war with Iran before it, would soon surface. The cost was not in buildings or bridges, but to the people themselves.

A United Nations embargo prohibited all trade and financial transactions with Iraq except for food, medicine and relief supplies. Despite that, I visited the city's main teaching hospital and found it pitifully ill-equipped; not because medical equipment was included on the sanctions list, but, according to the government, there weren't the funds to buy what was needed. (Iraq was banned from selling its main export, oil.)

On the streets inflation was rampant and rationing of food was in place. Anyone who could speak English questioned why the West continued to punish the Iraqi people so. We also recorded people – selected at random and not by our constant minders – echoing the belief that Iraq had historic rights to Kuwait and would one day retake it. Sanctions-busting appeared to keep the local markets afloat; in one meat store I found New Zealand lamb which had been destined for Jordan and had found its way here.

After a few days there it struck me how much the West had misread Iraq; how there had been the ill-founded belief that ordinary, war-weary Iraqis would rise up against their leader. I even came across minority Coptics (Middle East Christians) who supported his brutal oppression of the Marsh Arabs and Kurds. Their belief was that only Saddam could provide stability in Iraq. There were also those who furtively condemned Saddam.

But why, given what they have collectively been through, would the Iraqi people keep the leader who had visited such misery on them? Iraq is a country with a long history of advanced civilisation, it has both an educated work force and vast oil wealth. I was baffled. I later read analyses by Iraqi exiles pointing to why the West had so misunderstood the politics of Iraq; of why journalists like me were so perplexed. The conclusion was that Saddam was in fact a product of Iraqi society; that his rule not only depended on brutality but also on the submissiveness of many of his subjects and the sort of active support I'd witnessed.

In February 1993 there was an overriding sense of intimidation. Saddam's poster was everywhere and there was a well-founded fear of his secret police. Through the media, he was in an absolute position to manipulate opinion about the outside world.

The attack on the Al Rashid Hotel just a fortnight before we had checked in as guests had sparked outrage. Foreign journalists there at the time were among the injured. Saddam used the opportunity to visit them in hospital and pronounce once more that the West always bombs civilian targets.

The Kiwi team involved in the destruction of chemical weapons had been on the receiving end of that public outrage. They told me of incidents of their vehicles being stoned and of constant intimidation by the authorities. Richard Malone and I also had a small taste of it at a restaurant, where a man stormed up to our table. I thought he was going to hit us. Instead, he emptied a bottle of water over our food, ruining it.

We should not be surprised, the oleaginous Minister of Information told me in an interview that took days to arrange. People were being punished unfairly by the West, he claimed.

For all that, we met with little in the way of hostility. There was a sort of resigned indifference towards us on the streets. We were mostly left alone as we filmed in the market

The Road to Baghdad

places and even at the extraordinary shrine to the war of attrition against Iran. It is a soaring structure of two hands holding enormous crossed swords. At their base, dozens of helmets from the war dead are captured in large nets.

But I always had the sense that we were being watched; the feeling that our rooms at the Al Rashid were bugged and possibly videoed through a two-way mirror.

There were distinct limitations on what we could do and where we could go. For instance, we were refused permission to film at the site where the chemical weapons were being destroyed. But there were a few small victories. We were supposed to buy Iraqi currency at the official rate, which was $US3 for one Iraqi dinar. On the black market, we bought 35 dinars for one dollar!

It was worth the risk for those of us just passing through, but Western journalists stationed there had no choice but to play it by the book and buy at the official rate. It made for some gross disparities. One evening over dinner at the Al Rashid I ordered a bottle of wine which cost around $US30 – expensive enough. Sharing the meal with us was an American TV producer based semi-permanently in Baghdad. On buying the second bottle of wine, he ruefully entreated us to "enjoy it guys. That bottle of wine has just cost me a thousand bucks!"

The Al Rashid was one of the most famous landmarks in Baghdad during the Gulf War. It was from here that journalists like CNN's Peter Arnett had beamed live during the height of the allied bombing. We arrived to find the whole wall in front of the lobby covered in sheets of plastic. A US Tomahawk missile had landed just outside, leaving a huge crater in the ground and demolishing much of an outside wall. Two receptionists were killed. It was one of those hotels like the Hotel Split in Croatia, the Intercontinental in Zagreb and the Holiday Inn in Sarajevo that held a certain mystique. It was a journalists' hotel; history was made and reported from here.

Interestingly, work had just begun on a mosaic of former President George Bush at the very entrance to the hotel. Later, a caption in English and Arabic would be added saying "Bush is criminal." The idea was that anyone entering or leaving the hotel would be forced to tread on the ex-president's face.

Our Information Ministry minder had spent part of his childhood in the United States and was able to translate the unreasonable behaviour of his leader into the reasoned English of a New England school teacher. He, too, I later discovered, would fall foul of the paranoid internal security service and lose his job. Certainly, his lasting achievement for me was to secure a watch featuring the face of the Great Leader himself – the ultimate one-up on a Mickey Mouse watch.

We left the way we came, in the back of a GMC jeep. It was something of a relief to escape the relentless oppression of the place, but we had one more job to do. I wanted to capture a sense of the menace of Iraq and the best place to do that was at the border post. There was no chance of us openly filming, we would have to shoot covertly. Richard and I discussed at length whether we could or couldn't manage it. We settled on an idea of masking the camera with tape to disguise anything that might indicate it was on and rolling. A wide-angle lens meant that Richard could carry it in a casual fashion and still capture the action of the border search and interrogation. We were nervous – desperately so. To be caught and charged with spying could carry a ten-year sentence. We got away with it, and those pictures made for some of the most dramatic coverage of my feature story for *Holmes*.

A SPORTING LIFE

What You Don't Hear

Liam Jeory

There were times when the position of European Correspondent might more accurately have been entitled Sporting Correspondent. It really brings home just how important sport is to the New Zealand psyche when I add up the sporting tours and competitions I have covered between 1988 and '95. One America's Cup, one Admiral's Cup, two Kiwi rugby league tours of Great Britain, two All Black tours of South Africa and England/Scotland, two rugby World Cups, one women's rugby World Cup, one Whitbread Round the World race, one Commonwealth Games, three Badminton horse trials, three Wembley league grand finals, one squash world championship, two British Squash Opens, and one Kiwi cricket tour of England.

Sport always provides a contrast with normal reporting. For starters, you are usually dealing with excellence, and with people who truly do New Zealand proud.

The 1988 America's Cup, more commonly called the "big-boat" campaign, was my first taste of big-time sporting competition. The whole thing was a massive PR exercise, because never has there been a more one-sided competition. It didn't matter if the big boat was the fastest monohull yacht in the world, it was never going to win against Dennis Conner's catamaran. Consequently, the real action was never on the water, it was in the press.

The most famous moment of that campaign came at the final press conference. Now the true story of how that was filmed and got to air can be told. TVNZ and Channel Nine, this being the early days of our co-operative relationship, had arranged to share the filming, us from the back of the room, their camera to handle any shots from the front. Their cameraman was Drew Benjamin, who would later work with me throughout Europe.

At the end of the conference, after plenty of traded insults and ill feeling, the cameras were being packed up and the media were making their way out of the room when Dennis Conner, who'd arrived three sheets to the wind, made his famous "get off the stage, you're a loser, you're full of bullshit" comments to Bruce Farr. At the end of his little speech he turned to see the media trooping out, most having missed the exchange. Then he looked down to where Drew was standing beneath him, having caught the whole thing on tape. Conner's fixed smile dropped, Drew's didn't. It just got wider. He made a "Thanks mate, I got that" comment and what may well have been an unrecorded spat became worldwide news.

In August 1989 I was sent to cover the Admiral's Cup in Cowes, on the Isle of Wight. It was quite an assignment because my crew and I were staying with the New Zealand team in one of their two rented houses. We bunked down just like the crews, sharing three to a room, plus our gear and editing equipment. It took a bit of getting used to, for us as journalists living with our subjects, and for them, no doubt, living with journalists. But once they knew that Drew was the same man who sprang Dennis Conner, well, we were in.

There were occasions when being so close was positively beneficial, like the time the French protested the Kiwis for a sail allegedly touching them, a big no no. But we had filmed the whole incident, and when asked were able to set up our video gear before the protest jury and prove that it never happened. That may well have been the difference between the subsequent third place and no place at all.

What You Don't Hear

When the fleet took off for its first overnight race of the Cup, I took the shore crew for dinner, by way of a thank-you for providing us with on-the-water transport around the race courses, and for the care back at our lodgings. One drink led to another until someone decided we should make a video of what the mice get up to when the cats are away.

The video has gone down in yachting legend with the sight of some of New Zealand yachting's better known identities at the kitchen sink cleaning Vegemite stains out of the crew's undies, prancing around the stove with nothing on but aprons and big smiles, and culminating in a mass orgy in the crew's mess room, although I hasten to add it wasn't for real.

Somehow word of the video got out, and soon we were the toast of Cowes, invited to all the best parties. We thought it was because we were nice guys, until they told us to make sure we brought our video. Bootleg copies are still being aired around Auckland to this day.

One day a larger-than-life character by the name of Aran Hansen took us for a spin across the Solent to meet the Russians. They'd just arrived with their yacht, *Fazisi*, to compete in their first ever Whitbread Round the World race. Aran was keen to enjoy their launching party.

When we arrived we were introduced to a Russian who went by the nickname of Crocodile. "Oh yeah," said Aran. "My name's Whale." At 140 kilos, that was obvious to us. But Crocodile asked why. Aran filled his mouth with beer, tilted his head back and blew a perfect spout. The Russians thought it was hilarious, and the party began.

When time came for toasts, it was multicultural. "Cheers" from the English, "Prosit" from the Germans, "????" from the Russians, and "Shit yeah" from Whale. When the Russians asked if that was a Kiwi drinking toast, Aran replied "Shit yeah" and proceeded to work on getting their pronunciation correct.

Four months later at Christmas I came home to New Zealand for a holiday. The Whitbread fleet was in town, and I went along to the pub for a beer. It was crowded with sailors and from a corner I heard much laughter, clinking of glasses and very loud "Shit yeahs". There was Crocodile and the rest of the Russians, in New Zealand, toasting all and sundry and unable to figure out why no-one was responding in kind.

The 1989 Kiwi rugby league tour of Great Britain is memorable, not so much for anything the Kiwis did, but rather the behaviour of my colleagues from *One World of Sport*. Grant Nisbett was the commentator and Gavin Service the producer, dividing their time between the 1989 All Blacks in Wales, and the concurrent Kiwi tour in the north of England.

Keen followers of horse flesh, they were always on for a flutter. They would place a bet in Dover, pick up the winnings in Exeter, place another few bets in Gloucester, drive on a few more miles and check on the results at Stratford. And so on they travelled between the tours. They must have done all right, because they always arrived with a smile on their faces. Except in Hull.

It was a cold and windy night in Hull when the Kiwis played. It ought to have been memorable for the fact that they had arranged a little something with the ref. Their physio, Peter Boyle, or Boiler to his mates, was forever running on and off the field tending to players, passing on info and what have you. Finally the ref, in a staged fit of pique, blew the game up and ordered Boiler off the field to have an early shower. He didn't know, in fact no-one knew, what he'd done wrong, or if the ref even had the right to banish him. To everyone's amusement, though, he went.

Unfortunately, in Hull the crowd have a nasty little trick. If their side is losing, as it was this night, they start throwing coins. Our commentary setup was between the stand and the sideline, and we were a prime target. A well thrown coin doesn't just hurt, it can draw blood. And for much of the second half we were under attack. I've never been back to Hull. And I never got to see that tour out. I was sent off to cover the fall of the Berlin Wall.

Every year a favourite event was the Badminton horse trials. To appreciate just how good New Zealanders are at equestrianism, you only have to see how respected they are at

Badminton. This is an event where Princess Anne, the Queen, Prince Philip et al usually attend. And it was the likes of Mark Todd, Blyth Tait, Vicki Latta and Andrew Nicholson who reigned supreme.

I was privileged to see what those who know the sport describe as one of the finest feats of horsemanship ever. Mark Todd hadn't been doing too well on his horse. Then a fellow competitor, injured and unable to ride, asked Todd to take his horse, The Irishman, around the cross-country. Todd not only took a strange horse around the course, but he did so in a record time with the only clear run. The next day he could have won except he clipped one jump and finished third. It was incredible riding.

The next year he didn't do so well. In fact, after one round, he was distinctly unhappy. But he discovered a new way of letting the media know. As the New Zealand journalists gathered around, a hot and sweaty Mark Todd picked up his young daughter and prepared to answer the inevitable question. It fell to me to ask him "how he felt at this minute". Mark barely started speaking before his daughter grabbed his riding crop and brought it down fair square across my face. Todd was mortified, my fellow journalists were hysterical, and I could only say, "I get the point."

I'd never seen women's rugby when I was asked to cover the semis and finals of the women's rugby World Cup being held in Wales in April 1991. It was the first time a women's representative rugby team had been selected and sent overseas. What I expected and what I found were two different things. I expected large, lumbering and, to be honest, unattractive females playing amateurish rugby. What I found were very feminine, attractive women, professionally coached and playing to an exceptionally high standard.

The New Zealand women, unfortunately, lost the final to the United States. Afterwards I hung around outside the dressing room waiting for interviews. Now most sports teams are comfortable to invite the media into their changing rooms after a good win or at the end of a tour. The women were no different. So imagine my surprise when I was told not to stand around outside. "Come on in, we're not shy if you're not." I could barely hold Drew back.

I wish I could tell you what a great time I had in there. But the minute I walked into the hot, steamy atmosphere my glassed fogged up totally, as did the camera lens. We couldn't see a thing. But it was a highlight for me to be invited to the team's end-of-tour party, to receive a thank-you for taking some interest. If only all teams were as pleasant.

I'd never covered an All Black tour when they arrived in Britain to defend their world title in October 1991. It didn't take long to find out that this team was different from those I'd covered before. Not so much unfriendly as distant. Pleasant as individuals; as a team, quite rude.

Early on in the tour I was sitting in the lounge waiting for my crew when the team doctor, John Mayhew, came over and invited me to dinner. It was to be just him and us, and a couple of others – nothing to do with the All Blacks. I told my crew and we all went off to get freshened up and came back at the appointed time. John came over with an embarrassed look and said the dinner was off. It transpired that a couple of the players had decided to come, then a few more, and finally most of the team. John was told he had to uninvite me.

I was as embarrassed as Doc; I hadn't asked to go, I'd been asked. The next morning Alex Wyllie took me aside and said, "I heard about last night. That was bloody rude. It wasn't my decision but I'm offering an apology."

After that experience, perhaps I shouldn't have been surprised at what I witnessed in Dublin before the loss to Australia in the semi-finals. The All Blacks were training at a local school and hundreds of young boys were on the sidelines watching. I interviewed a group who told me they'd wagged class to watch the All Blacks. "The best in the world," they told me. No sooner had I finished filming them when a group of players ran across to our side and started doing exercises on the ground.

"Good on yer All Blacks," yelled one of the boys I'd just spoken to. "Fuck off you little c***," one of the players snapped back. I don't know who was more shocked, me or the boys. But the look on their faces said it all. Perhaps it shouldn't have been surprising when the next day the sports editor of the *Irish Times* wrote how he'd been given the run around trying to get a simple interview with some of the team, and headlined his piece "Men of Steel, Hearts of Stone". He went on to write how "they'd rather have an enema than talk to a journalist".

Yet this same team, after the loss to Australia, was also capable of dignity, especially John Kirwan. We were all shell-shocked in the area outside the dressing rooms under the stand. The Australians were jubilant and eager to talk. The All Blacks had locked themselves in their room. Then John Kirwan came out, eyes still red, squared his shoulders and faced us all, giving a gracious and courageous performance when inside he must have been dying. Gary Whetton came out and did likewise. I was proud of them at that moment, despite all that had gone before.

It was quite a contrast to spend time with the Western Samoan team during that 1991 World Cup. Plenty has been written about how they were the darlings of the tournament. Perhaps an experience I had will illustrate why.

On the day of their greatest triumph, beating Argentina for a quarter-final berth, I joined the crowd outside waiting for the team to get on the bus. I joined a group of English rugby fans wearing Western Samoan colours. They told me how they'd sat in the pub one day and thrown a dart to decide what team they were going to support. The dart landed on Western Samoa and this group had followed the team to every game.

After the game, the Western Samoans invited us into the dressing room. It was deathly quiet. The team gathered in the middle and said a prayer. Only when the prayer was over did the hooting and hollering begin. It was great television, showing emotion one never sees, or is rarely allowed to see, with the All Blacks. Afterwards I was standing outside when one of the try scorers, the wing Timo Tagaloa, came up to me and asked, "How did I play, Liam?"

I told him he'd played great. Whereupon he gave me a

huge bear hug and said, "Thank-you. Thank-you." Such behaviour from a rugby player? Unprecedented. But then the Western Samoans were setting new precedents.

I found myself covering the All Blacks again the next year, this time to South Africa. It was the resumption of rugby ties, the beginning of a new era. That's not to say there was no controversy. The tour began in the shadow of a couple of Springboks being banned for taking steroids. I was asked to see if I could find out how widespread steroid use was among South African players.

To be frank, I didn't really know where to start looking, especially when everyone involved was keeping their mouths tightly shut. As I drove along the highway to our hotel, I saw a fitness centre among some trees, and figured it was as good a place as any to start. I went in and asked to see the manager. He was a body builder, with a big mouth. I told him straight what I was trying to find out, and couldn't believe my ears when he told me that many top rugby players worked out in his gym, and yes, he supplied quite a few of them with steroids. He wasn't so stupid that he would name names, but he told me everything else. Sometimes in life one is lucky.

The All Blacks arrived a few days later. The reception at the airport at midnight was incredible. The arrival hall was absolutely packed, the welcome ecstatic. The contrast with the Australians a week later was extreme. They may have been the world champions, and their arrival was at midday, but if there were a hundred people there to welcome them they would have been lucky. It was the clearest possible statement that, in South Africa, it's the All Blacks who matter.

My next oval ball tour was to England in 1993, first to cover the Kiwi league tour, and then to cross over and link up with the All Blacks for their tour of England and Scotland.

I have made my share of faux pas in my time. But my worst must have been at an aftermatch function in Wigan. I was making conversation with a young player when a woman wobbled past on high heels. She must have been fifty, with bleached blonde hair piled high, a low-cut sequined top and no evident support, a tight black leather skirt and red stockings.

What You Don't Hear

I almost choked and made some comment like "My gawd. Will. You. Look. At. That!" The young player muttered, "I have to. Every day. That's my mother." And he walked away.

When I wasn't embarrassing myself, I can lay claim to breaking the story about Inga the winger defecting to league. Not the rumours, but the final cold, hard proof that he was going. I was with the Kiwis in their Leeds hotel when I was given the word that Inga had signed on the dotted line. But, seeing as he was with the All Blacks and wanted to finish that tour first, he hadn't signed an actual contract. Instead he'd signed a letter of agreement to sign as soon as his rugby tour was over, or some similar instrument.

Having Graham Lowe on our commentary team meant confirmation was a breeze. He simply rang the right people in British rugby league, was given the proof and I had the story. The trouble is the All Black management simply pooh-poohed the story, as did other journalists travelling with them. No-one wanted to confront the possibility of facing up to it and having to kick Inga off the All Black tour. So when Inga said he hadn't signed a contract, they all believed him.

Inga announced his signing as soon as he returned to New Zealand. It annoyed me when in his subsequent book the All Black captain, Sean Fitzpatrick, claimed that the journalists all missed the biggest story of that tour, Inga's signing. If the All Blacks all knew about it during the tour, then those approached about it were certainly being less than truthful when they dismissed my report. But real journalism and reporting on All Black tours parted ways some years ago as far as I'm concerned.

Before I explain further, I have to make the distinction between the pride I feel for the All Blacks on the field, for the way they play the game and their incredible record, and reporting on the team off the field. I also have to make the distinction between the players as individuals, and the team.

The players, one on one, are, with a few exceptions, fine personable men, some quite hilarious when they're given the chance to express themselves. But put them together as a team, and add in the management mix which seeks to control them to the nth degree, and it's hard to find any journalist who would tell you they like covering a modern All Black tour.

The truth about an All Black tour is that, other than game day, it's dead boring. They're usually just day after day of attending practices, being yelled at to turn the bloody camera off, and trying not to offend the coach. It used to be that to interview a player, one only had to ask him. Now you have to ask the media liaison officer, who may or may not ask the player, who may or may not deign to reply. Being granted a simple interview has got to be as hard as gaining a royal audience.

For some people, though, evidently it isn't difficult. There was the occasion during the 1995 World Cup when the players wouldn't come out of their dressing room to speak to the journalists because they were having a sing along with Andrew Strong, the lead singer from the Irish movie *The Commitments*. Except this Andrew Strong was an imposter. After he was publicly exposed the All Black management was scrambling to deny it was ever taken in. The Andrew Strong imposter has some All Black team gear to prove otherwise.

It's a sad fact of New Zealand sporting journalism that to say one doesn't love travelling with the All Blacks, to criticise the holy grail, is probably to invite the cold shoulder and finish forever one's chances of covering another of their tours. But what the heck? There are always other teams, like the Western Samoans.

In fact, when asked to cover the 1995 World Cup I said I would only go if I could travel with the Western Samoans. They remind one it is possible to report a rugby tour and enjoy it.

Sporting Tales

Cameron Bennett

Yachting is a pastime I've always steered clear of. Not because of a lack of interest; I've always thought that sailing around the world would be the ultimate romantic dream. My reason is simple – I get horrendously seasick. So it was with some trepidation that I approached coverage of the start of the Whitbread yacht race out of Southampton in September 1993.

It was a yachties' heaven at the Southampton marina; the finest ocean-going yachts in the world and the finest sailors. Taking pride of place, of course, were the New Zealand boats; Grant Dalton's mighty maxi *New Zealand Endeavour*, Chris Dixon's *Tokio*, Brad Butterworth in the unlikely role of co-skippering *Winston* with a lumbering Dennis Conner and Ross Field's *Yamaha*.

In the days leading up to the race start, tape editor and cameraman Brendan Donohoe and I filed previews. As far as I was concerned, the yachties were welcome to it; their boats were just empty racing shells of fibreglass and other composites. But that's the sort of naive observation you keep to yourself on occasions like this. We had our mobile edit pack in our hotel room and from there set about producing more informed observations. There was a large contingent of TVNZ staff, too, which really added to the event for me – not least that the irrepressible Pete Montgomery could help fill the gaps in my knowledge.

On race day itself the Southampton marina was a sea of colour and excitement. Television crews stalled skippers for last-minute interviews; wellwishers cheered from the wharfside; crew members clung to loved ones. There seemed to be a uniform blondeness to the wives and girlfriends, as I recall.

But if they were overcome with emotion, I had problems of my own; like, how was I going to cover this event? The obvious choice was to board one of the many press boats, but there had to be something better. Lurking in the back of my mind was Liam's coverage of the last event, which not only reeked of a yachtie who knew what he was talking about, but also that he'd managed a piece-to-camera in a rubber Zodiac while dodging in and out of the flotilla.

Given my naivete in matters nautical, I presumed I would have to be on board one of the boats as she crossed the line if my coverage was going to be worthwhile. It wasn't till later that I found out that no-one, certainly journalists, even contemplated doing that. It just wasn't done – not here, anyway.

My prayers were answered by Murray Taylor, a Kiwi involved with the Yamaha promotion. Brendan and I were hurriedly kitted out in the boat's colours and climbed aboard the sleek 60-footer in the knowledge that we'd jump off into a support boat shortly before the gun. I must confess to feeling a terrible fraud, in my team jacket, as we pulled out from the wharf amidst the flag-waving and cheers.

We were one of the first away. Ross Field had decided there was no point in waiting out the dockside farewells. We pitched about in the Solent, tacking this way and that and the rest of the fleet joined us, along with hundreds of spectator craft. Close to time, the waters were boiling from the chop whipped up by the fleet, and still no sign of our support boat. All around, these superb yachts all jostled and jibed for the best wind advantage. I watched *New Zealand Endeavour* slicing by close to our stern – an awesome sight. The scene was dramatic in a way no TV coverage I had seen was really able to show.

Ross Field had been relaxed until those last few minutes, but then it was as if someone flipped a switch; he and the crew were tense and fired up.

TVNZ was due to call Ross on a mobile phone he'd stowed in his all-weather jacket. But this was no time to lose concentration; he handed it to me. The race hadn't started yet but it certainly looked like it. Orders were barked out, the crew scurried like clockwork and I recorded a quick standup in those last couple of minutes before the gun.

And then, the most gruelling yacht race in the world was under way. In those few moments I knew what all the fuss was about. What I didn't know was where to put myself without getting in the way. I made for the central hatch. Perching there was all very well until the first change of sail. In what seemed like the blink of an eye the crew had whipped down a soaking sheet and proceeded to cram it through the central hatch – on top of me. About the same moment, the cellphone started ringing; TVNZ were expecting to cross live to Ross Field.

But in my flurry to escape being swamped by the sail, the cellphone had fallen out of my pocket and was somewhere in *Yamaha's* bilges. When it started ringing again I crawled on all fours from under the sail, making my way to where I thought the sound was coming from. Through all of this *Yamaha* was pitching and yawing, and I was feeling increasingly queasy. I found the phone in a dark recess at the stern just in time; Jane Dent was on the line all set to go live. If Ross Field wasn't available, I would do as second best.

I clambered back above decks and launched into the cross with Pete Montgomery-like gusto, which took my mind off a growing wave of nausea.

Next the Zodiac arrived. It was about time; we had all but made the English Channel and the next stop was Punta del Este in Uruguay. By now *Yamaha* was heeling hard under a strong wind and pulling some 16 knots. The idea was to wait until the Zodiac caught the rise of a swell and was more or less level with the yacht, and then jump in. Easier said than done with a television camera and equipment, but Brendan and I managed it. Ross Field and his crew barely noticed we'd gone, they were concentrating that hard.

To have been seasick aboard *Yamaha* would have been the ultimate display of poor form; but there was no holding back aboard the Zodiac – I heaved my heart out.

Back in Southampton that night, we ran into a bunch of professional yachting writers who were chewing over the day's events. A well-known American writer was gloating over how well his press boat had done in pursuing the fleet; there had been none other quite so adept at avoiding the marine police, apparently. That was my cue. "I don't know about the writing game, but in television you have to be on board one of the boats for the best coverage. *Yamaha* worked out brilliantly." There was a look of incredulity. "You were on *Yamaha* for the start of the race?" So put out was the American that he said he'd be making an official enquiry. He was sure it was against the rules.

Brendan's pictures of the event were some of the most outstanding of the day. Our report would go on to pick up a Qantas sports award. Not bad for a couple of landlubbers.

Sports assignments were more often than not an ordeal for me; I could be more nervous about covering an All Black match than I was going into a war zone.

My interests have tended to be elsewhere, and my experience of covering games was largely confined to the B-grade and below, as a cub reporter in Whangarei. As TVNZ's Europe Correspondent the only games I covered were internationals. If it wasn't the All Blacks, it was the Silver Ferns or Mark Todd at Badminton or Paul Radisich in his touring car at Donnington or Monza.

I knew full well that sport, like nothing else, impassioned viewers at home. It was unnerving knowing that a small army of experts would be sitting in their armchairs watching for any error. One slip up on the run count, one player mistaken for another and there would be hell to pay.

My first outing with the All Blacks was not game

coverage but the celebrated wedding in Treviso, Italy, of John Kirwan in November 1991. The setting was tranquil; the atmosphere was not, if you were a TVNZ reporter. Having just lost the World Cup the Men in Black were not at their most light-hearted. Still, this was a "good news" story and I wasn't expecting any problem.

I'd flown down to Italy from London with bureau cameraman Phil Hanna. I'd come expecting they'd be co-operative, and why not? They were well aware of the value of publicity and the importance of an event like this for their fans.

I didn't expect to be treated with such disdain and it left me with a sour taste. We got our story in the end, but it was disappointing the way we had to get it.

Perhaps the likes of the All Blacks do get overloaded with publicity, perhaps all the hype over-inflates their egos, deifies them beyond what they actually are – footballers. In my time away, I found myself groping to find a perspective for sport and sports stars. The job forced that; one minute you could be covering a Middle East peace summit, the next you're reporting on a ball sport. Which was the most important: a birdie on the ninth or a breakthrough in negotiations over the West Bank? In television terms, there is a simple answer to that: sport outrates Yasser Arafat. My own feeling is that sport can be elevated beyond itself; that players, no matter how talented, tough and competitive they may be, and the public can be led into believing that a game is more than just a game. I discovered, in places like Bosnia, heroes of a different ilk whose courage goes unsung and unrewarded; who are not playing games but are playing for real. I had found my perspective.

For all that, I count it as a privilege to have met and watched in action some of our finest sportspeople. Take Mark Todd and his remarkable ability with a horse – any horse it seems. I have never seen anyone able to strike up a rapport with an animal in quite the way he can, whether it's a horse or a dog. It seemed to be a "feel" thing. When we filmed him in training, there appeared to be little spoken communication with the horse. It just seemed to know what he wanted from it;

a gentle nudge here or movement of the rein there. No shouting, no histrionics. In Britain he was regarded as the consummate horseman; his ability to combine that special affinity with horses and determined sportsmanship was unsurpassed.

There was the indomitable Peter Blake. I covered his departure and return from the Jules Verne round-the-world-non-stop challenge. Another consummate sportsman and diplomat.

And there was Annelise Coberger. I was covering the Winter Olympics in Albertville, France, in Febuary 1992, when the 20-year-old from Christchurch took silver in the women's slalom. She was the first athlete from the southern hemisphere to win a winter medal. It was high excitement. I met up with Annelise several times during my tour and was increasingly struck by how young and lonely she seemed on one of the world's most punishing circuits. She'd been skiing professionally since she was 18. To reach her ranking as a medallist in 1992 and second in the World Cup standings the following year had cost her every summer since she was a child. There was the constant pressure to perform; particularly after taking the World Cup women's slalom win in Austria and the silver medal in rapid succession. But in terms of glamour – there wasn't any to speak of. Just a string of cramped hotel rooms lined with wet ski gear and the drive to the next event. By the Winter Olympics of 1994, I noticed that Annelise did not exude the commitment and hunger of a champion. She was already looking for something else from life. I wasn't surprised to hear that she'd decided to quit the circuit in March this year, aged 23.

For me, those 1994 Winter Olympics in Norway were the most rewarding sports event I covered. I wasn't operating on my own this time; my colleague Paul Cutler had come up from Auckland to produce. Being part of a small team made all the difference for me; it helped make the Games.

Lillehammer was a much more compact and manageable venue than Albertville. This was a small country putting on a big event, and, right from its stunning opening, it never lost its special, friendly atmosphere and sense of promise. Apart from the great names of winter sport there was the sideshow of Nancy Kerrigan and Tonya Harding, the two American princesses of ice skating. At times the sideshow took over. On a couple of occasions cameraman Brendan Donohoe and I were assigned to the story. There were that many camera crews at the skating rink that we couldn't get a look in. Our story became the US media overkill. It became an angle for the US networks too: I appeared on an ABC sports show for a brief soundbite. It had been preceded by "Even in far away Noo Zealand they're interested . . ."

Outside, the weather plummeted to 30C below. To remove your scarf and breathe the air unfiltered at times burnt your lungs like cigarette smoke. We put together features on the Norwegian hosts. Many of them were camping in the sub-zero temperatures. The campsites had the look of Mount Maunganui at Christmas; there were deck chairs and open-air barbecues. The difference was that the tent pegs had been driven into pack ice, and to leave clothes outside overnight was to find them frozen solid in the morning.

Sports cover makes up a large part of the year for TVNZ's man in Europe; from British Open golf to cricket and rugby league. The intricacies of cricket as a game have always eluded me, so I have much to thank *One Network News* sports editor Richard Becht for in nursing me, long-distance, through tours by the Kiwi squad.

Though interested in sport, I'm not passionate about it. My Australian colleagues in the London bureau soon discovered that, when their jokes at the expense of Kiwi sports stars got no rise out of me, clearly, the new TVNZ man in London did not share his predecessor's enthusiasm.